Dominic Fuge

Foreword by Dr Julian Davies

THE ESSENTIAL GUIDE TO UCAS PERSONAL STATEMENTS

trotman | t

The Essential Guide to UCAS Personal Statements

This first edition published in 2025 by Trotman, an imprint of Trotman Indigo Publishing Ltd, 18e Charles Street, Bath BA1 1HX

© Trotman Indigo Publishing Ltd 2025

Author: Dominic Fuge

British Library Cataloguing in Publication Data
A catalogue record for this book is available from the British Library.

Paperback ISBN 978-1-911724-62-9
eISBN 978-1-911724-63-6

All rights reserved. This book is sold subject to the condition that it shall not, by way of trade or otherwise, be lent, resold, hired out or otherwise circulated without the publisher's prior written consent in any form of binding or cover other than that in which it is published and without a similar condition including this condition being imposed on the subsequent purchaser. No part of this publication may be reproduced, stored in a retrieval system or transmitted in any form or by any means, electronic and mechanical, photocopying, recording or otherwise without prior permission of Trotman Indigo Publishing.

Every effort has been made to trace copyright holders and to obtain their permission for the use of copyright material. The publisher apologises for any errors or omissions, and would be grateful to be notified of any corrections that should be incorporated in future editions of this book.

The authorised representative in the EEA is Easy Access System Europe Oü (EAS), Mustamäe tee 50, 10621 Tallinn, Estonia.

Printed and bound in the UK by 4Edge Ltd, Hockley, Essex

All details in this book were correct at the time of going to press. To keep up to date with all the latest news and updates and to access the online resources that accompany this book, use this QR code or visit www.trotman.co.uk/pages/the-essential-guide-to-ucas-personal-statements-resources

Endorsements

'Practical, accessible and clear – the best support after your teacher.'
Melrose Fernandes, Head of EAP and UCAS Adviser at Kings Education.

'An engaging read that guides students to writing a strong and authentic personal statement!'
Ellen Kuppersmith, Independent Educational Consultant, Owner – College Kupp.

'This essential guide unlocks the complexities of the university application process and reveals the secrets to writing a compelling personal statement.'
Chris Couch, Head of Careers & University Advising at Latymer Upper School, London.

'Rooted in real experience, guides like this offer valuable insight and support to students on their journey.'
Phillip Wenturine, Director of University Counseling at Brewster Madrid and CEO at Right Fit Future.

'*The Essential Guide to UCAS Personal Statements* by Dominic Fuge is the reassuring voice every student (and University Counsellor) needs when navigating the often overwhelming world of UK university applications. This impressively detailed evidence-based guide is the result of years of Fuge's insider expertise and experience; he transforms the personal statement from a source of stress into a confident, compelling showcase of student potential.'
Beverly Conway, IB DP Literature Language Teacher, College Counsellor and 11C Mentor.

'The book all advisers should advise to read.'
Elisabetta Incollingo, UCAS & Careers Advisor, St. Andrew's College Cambridge.

'An invaluable resource for families and advisers navigating the UCAS process.'
> Robert Ramey, Director of College Counseling at the British International School of Washington.

'Utterly spectacular! An informative and engaging read for anyone wanting to produce a winning UCAS personal statement and understand UK university applications.'
> Jason Brooks, Director of the Supercurricular Department at Oxford International College.

'Bravo! Dominic's extensive experience shines through in this tremendously comprehensive guide offering valuable advice for writing the UCAS personal statement, supported by helpful examples and insightful analysis. Dominic provides excellent guidance on considering course options, and future careers along with useful data and relevant commentary on the use of AI. This guide is a "must read" for any student aspiring to apply to a UK university, and I will certainly be recommending it to my students.'
> Rhonda Leshman, University and Futures Counselor, Barcelona High School.

'Supportive, clear and practical, this guide helps students confidently navigate UK university admissions. With thoughtful advice on course selection, super-curricular exploration, and self-reflection, it empowers students to tell their stories with pride and purpose. It's a must-have for families and counselors alike.'
> Bernadette Condesso, Director of School & College Counseling, Gulliver Prep (Miami, FL).

'A comprehensive and easy-to-understand guide for students and parents about higher education in the UK. Dominic breaks down the lengthy and complex application process and career path into simple, easy-to-follow steps.'
> Zul Enkhsaikhan, Student Counselor, Orchlon International School.

'An engaging and well-researched guide that reads as if a trusted adviser is walking students through each step. Clear, practical, and full of genuinely useful resources, especially for those navigating the UK system from abroad.'

Marian Alvarez Calderon, University Counsellor, San Silvestre School, Lima, Peru.

Contents

	Endorsements	iii
	Figures and tables	ix
	About the author	xi
	Acknowledgements and dedications	xiii
	Foreword by Dr Julian Davies	xv
	Preface	xix
1|	**Introduction and background**	**1**
	It really is about making it attention-grabbing (and how to use this book)	1
	Why UCAS has changed the personal statement format (and does it matter?)	7
	The higher education landscape of UK universities	13
2|	**Finding your right course**	**18**
	Vocational vs. subject passion	18
	Ways to conduct research (and which types of degrees are available)	22
	Creating your university shortlist	29
3|	**Developing your super-curricular profile**	**34**
	What's available?	34
	Work experience is achievable for all	41
	Recording and writing reflectively about your super-curricular activities	50
4|	**The writing**	**56**
	Tackling question 1: 'Why do you want to study this course or subject?'	56
	Tackling question 2: 'How have your qualifications and studies helped you to prepare for this course or subject?'	63
	Tackling question 3: 'What else have you done to prepare outside of education, and why are these experiences helpful?'	65

5 | After writing — 68
Stepping away and then stepping forward — 68
Finally submitting — 71
Really knowing your personal statement, especially if you might be interviewed — 77

6 | Opportunities and challenges of using AI — 79

7 | Personal statement examples — 84
Example 1: Geography — 85
Commentary on Example 1 — 86
Example 2: Medicine — 92
Commentary on Example 2 — 93
Example 3: Economics — 98
Commentary on Example 3 — 99
Example 4: Philosophy — 104
Commentary on Example 4 — 105
Example 5: Architecture — 110
Commentary on Example 5 — 111
Example 6: Computer Science — 114
Commentary on Example 6 — 115

Figures and tables

Figures

1	An overview of the main criteria UK universities use to assess undergraduate applications before making an interview offer/conditional offer.	2
2	Common clichés to avoid in your personal statement writing.	5
3	University choice caveats to consider when making your selection of five courses.	19
4	Preferences that students may have when selecting their universities.	23
5	A breakdown of co-curricular experiences (extra-curricular and super-curricular).	36
6	Super-curricular tick list.	40
7	The process of securing speculative work experience.	45
8	CV template example.	47
9	Cover letter structure.	48
10	A snippet from an exemplar personal statement (highlighting super-curricular variety and adequate reflection).	54
11	Possible sentence starters for reflections in the personal statement.	55
12	Eight ways to make your personal statement stand out.	60
13	Examples of possible crystallising moments drawing you to your chosen university course (which can be expanded on in the personal statement).	61
14	Breaking down the PEEL structure with a paragraph example.	62
15	A checklist when assessing personal statements (imagining being an admissions tutor).	69

Tables

1	Number of UCAS applicants in a 20-year sample, a steady increase.	3
2	A timeline for UCAS applications.	6
3	Vocational vs. Subject Passion Matrix.	21
4	Examples of some 'vocational' and 'subject passion' university course choices.	21
5	The 27 UK universities, divided by prestigious group.	24
6	Some recommended websites for university research.	28
7	University research table for students – 'reach', 'safe' and 'match' choices.	32
8	Applied and speculative work experience.	43
9	Work experience companies contact spreadsheet.	49
10	The various types of work experience.	49
11	A reflective journal for super-curricular activities.	52
12	A breakdown of the three personal statement questions.	59
13	How the personal statement examples link extra-curricular in Question 3 to suitability for the course and/or for university life.	66
14	Three companies that use the concept of reverse admissions.	75
15	Ways in which applicants can diversify their university course portfolio outside of the five course choices on UCAS.	76
16	Opportunities and challenges of AI for personal statement writing.	83

About the author

Dominic Fuge studied at three Russell Group universities – the University of Cambridge; University of Edinburgh; Durham University. He studied different subjects at each institution. While completing his GCSEs and A levels in London, Dominic found a deep interest in evolutionary biology, philosophical enquiry and the study of the past. He therefore travelled to the North East of England to read Archaeology and Anthropology. Following this, Dominic moved into the area of Psychology, wanting to research more about evolutionary psychopathology. He graduated from the University of Edinburgh with a master's degree in the Psychology of Mental Health, before studying Education at the University of Cambridge. Having undertaken such a broad range of subject areas at university level, this has shaped Dominic's views about just how flexible and transferable degrees can be for a wealth of different career areas and job opportunities. This has naturally influenced his approach when guiding, informing and advising school students – choose a subject area based on a combination of academic curiosity, subject passion and a consideration of the transferable skills gained.

The first job in education Dominic secured was teaching A level Psychology, while also supporting students who had learning or behavioural difficulties. This was at an inner-city state school in London. Subsequently, Dominic worked at two leading boarding schools in Oxford, where he steadily cultivated a reputation for effective line management and the pioneering of innovative methods to enhance university application strategies and careers learning. Dominic held the role of Head of University Engagement and Alumni Relations at Oxford International College. He also developed strategies for the oldest school in England to have taught the International Baccalaureate, known as St Clare's

Oxford. Now based in Cambridge since 2024, Dominic became the founding Head of Careers and Higher Education for Cardiff Sixth Form College Cambridge. This is a new branch of the original Cardiff site, known for consistently being ranked no. 1 in the UK for A level results.

Dominic is also interested in the world of business, and while an undergraduate student at Durham University, he joined an initiative designed to help students create their own businesses (called the Blueprint Enterprise Programme). He has since established two businesses – one of which donated to Durham University in 2022 and provided 100% scholarships for state school students to join educational programmes. In his spare time, Dominic enjoys whatever he can gain from travel, culture and good food. He also enjoys the occasional clay pigeon shooting and horse riding, as well as spending time with friends and family in the UK and beyond.

Feel free to contact the author, using his LinkedIn account www.linkedin.com/in/dominicfuge.

Acknowledgements and dedications

For my two incredible parents, Edward and Shiela, who were instrumental support in, among many things, my own journey to university. For my amazing girlfriend, Alice. We actually met during our postgraduate studies, even though we were both at Durham University for our undergraduate degrees and found out that we rented the exact same house at slightly different times while students there! For also Alice's family, who, along with many lovely experiences, have welcomed me with their 'Italianity' – Nino, Cinzia and Fede. Here's to some undergraduate friends that I am still very much in contact with (Paula, Aaron and Callum) and postgraduate friends (Freddie, Kelly, Chantal, Tianyi, Ekin, Dani, Elliot, Molly, Justin, Josh, Shana, Mario, Hailey, Alissa and Thibault). For also some wonderful old colleagues from the education sector who are now even greater friends (Jason, Dan, Laura, Massimo, Matt, Lucy, Kiran, Andy, Daniel, Shukor, Louise, Cesca and Rafi). Why not also a mention for some ancient and thus very long-standing friends, who were with me way back at high school in London (David, Julz and Michael)! Wishing Michael and Tara all the good fortune that comes with their newborn baby, Eden.

The process of preparing for university and even going to school is a tangibly formative part of development, and it has been great to keep in contact with my own A level Psychology teacher and Head of Sixth Form, Laura. It's been tremendous fun meeting for dinners and café visits and seeing her young daughter, Alba, grow up in Oxford.

I am still in my first year at Cardiff Sixth Form College, Cambridge, and I have enjoyed the regular evenings out and occasional gym visits (nothing too strenuous, of course!) with Jem and Steve from the College. What a fun experience it has been to share an office with Natalie and Hannah. I am fortunate to have probably one of the best line managers in the business, Chris Sweet!

Finally, of course, this book would not have been possible without the Trotman Indigo Publishing team. I first reached out with the proposal to Alexandra Price, who kept me in mind when a new book of this kind was ready to be published. It was really amazing to work with Alexandra and then subsequently Nicola Cattini, who both offered a lot of editorial insight, unwavering support and belief in this project from its earliest stages. Many thanks also to Louisa Smith, Claire Lawlor and Rani Race, who have also been instrumental.

Foreword
by Dr Julian Davies

If you are reading this as a young person looking ahead to university, I am envious of you. A great adventure awaits that I hope you enjoy and look back on with great fondness, as I do. I enjoyed my time at university so much that I went twice and spent a career in sixth form education helping students to make their own applications to university. Preparing for such applications is not something to do alone. You would be well advised to seek advice from your family, teachers and school advisors. This book will be an essential aid to you as it is written by an expert who understands the details of the application process and presents up-to-the-minute advice and guidance.

If there is some simple advice I have from my experience helping students, it is to give these decisions time and be truthful to yourself. For example, while at school myself, I did not feel I had a single, overarching career objective. I was rather envious of those who did and wondered how they *knew* that they wanted to be a doctor, lawyer or economist. It seemed impossible to have worked that out at age seventeen. Of course, it is entirely possible to have done so by then, but it is by no means essential, so don't worry if you haven't. I knew I wanted to go to university and I knew I enjoyed science, especially biology, with perhaps a leaning towards biochemistry. The answer did seem rather obvious to me, and that was to apply to universities that looked to have strong biology and biochemistry departments. In those days, that involved looking at hard copy prospectuses, and that is what I duly did. As for my personal statement, it was grounded in my interest in biology, and as a keen rugby player, in sport and extra-curricular activity. What followed was a shortlist and ultimately entry to the University of Bath to study Applied Biology. The 'Applied' component involved me selecting two external placements and I would advise you to consider university courses that offer this. The placements saw me spend six months working on molecular biology projects at an industrial placement in England and six months at the University of Illinois. So although I did not even begin to imagine my subsequent career in education when I applied to university, I nevertheless thoroughly enjoyed my studies and became much more self-dependent and confident after spending time in the real world of academic and industrial laboratories.

My route into education came about during my second stint at university. While undertaking research for my PhD, I topped up my funding through undergraduate laboratory supervision and A level personal tutoring. This is when I had my light bulb moment and realised that I was a teacher. So, if you are worried that you simply don't know what your career will be, I would advise you to follow your interest and choose a subject area that you enjoy and wish to spend more time studying. After that, your career may well find you.

After a number of years of classroom teaching, I moved to educational management and senior leadership, and I have spent the last 22 years running sixth form colleges. During this time, I have gained a good understanding of how best to help students prepare for their university applications and particularly the personal statement. You can find a great deal of advice of this nature in the pages of this book. From my perspective, I have found that students are well advised to spend time in Year 12, if not before, building evidence of their interest in their proposed university subject. As an example, students interested in engineering should read books written not for university-level study but for the layperson, about engineering. There is a wide range of such literature that is readily found with a quick internet search for 'Books for pre-university students on [insert subject name]'. In this way, easily accessible books can be found that will enable a student to immerse themselves and get a better understanding of their subject or perhaps of a specific area within their subject. I have heard it said that strong Oxbridge candidates should read twenty books before making their application. That may sound rather ambitious, but I agree with the notion that a student should self-discover more about their subject, independently of work covered in their school curriculum.

As principal of Cardiff Sixth Form College Cambridge, I have a student body of ambitious, able students who are seeking entry to the most competitive universities. I am fortunate that the author of this book, Dominic Fuge, is our Head of Careers and Higher Education and has overseen the development of a programme of super-curricular activities that provide many opportunities for students to develop a love, and depth of knowledge, of their subject. We call this programme, 'The Cambridge Edge'. One feature of this programme is that we ensure our students capture the new understandings in a diary. We call such things 'Insights'. The personal statement then becomes a recollection of insights from the student diary, gained over the past year or more. A strong statement would then link such insights to the student's own experiences to demonstrate a connection between deeper understandings of the subject and the preparedness of a student to study it. As an example, a student may have observed how medical staff work as a team and the role of the team leader, such as a medical consultant. The student may have seen how the consultant leads the team by listening carefully to the junior doctors and nurses and by giving clarity of direction. That student may then be able to draw a parallel to their own experiences in working within a team in school, perhaps in the debate club, and of any leadership roles they have had.

There are numerous ways to gain subject insights. Something I am very keen on is the direct observation of the work of experts in your chosen field. A classic way to do this is through work experience. If you are fortunate enough to have work experience, do keep a daily diary to ensure you don't forget the insights you note. I would also suggest that you be curious about the work you see. This could mean asking questions and trying to understand the challenges and solutions that are used. Work experience is often arranged through school or college, but I would also recommend that you be bold and seek out such experiences yourself. This may sound somewhat intimidating, but you may be surprised at how accommodating professional people will be if you contact them and politely inquire as to the possibility of making a visit to their place of work. Be mindful that such a person may take more kindly to your approach if they are hearing from a young person who tells them that they are as excited about their field of expertise as they are. Finally, don't forget that even the most preeminent Nobel Prize winner was once a 17-year-old wondering how they were going to win their place at university.

Many people look back on their time spent at university as being some of the best times of their lives. It is a time when you step well and truly out of your comfort zone, quite literally in fact, as you will likely spend university life away from your school friends and away from the comforts of family and home. The rewards, however, are life-changing and unforgettable. You will make new friends, often for life, engage in deeper study of your favourite academic discipline and become a more independent and self-reliant young adult.

As a school-age student looking towards university, the application process can be a daunting prospect. You face many decisions and will need to prepare before you apply. You'll need to decide on which universities to consider, perhaps in locations you have never visited before, and decide on a course from a list of thousands, including some that you may never have studied before, such as law or medicine. You need to research your chosen field, engage with the ideas in your subject beyond those studied in school and write a winning personal statement. This is where this book will help you. The author of this guide is an expert and an enthusiast in helping young people make successful applications to universities across the world. This book is a distillation of his advice and guidance. I'm sure you will benefit from its wisdom. Good luck and enjoy university!

Dr Julian Davies
Principal, Cardiff Sixth Form College Cambridge
March 2025

Preface

Possibly rather uniquely for an author, I have decided to write this preface first rather than at the end when the book has already been finalised. At the moment, as I sit at my newly-built desk within my studio apartment, based only a 20-second walk from the school where I work, not a single page has been written. Therefore, I am currently filled with excitement and enthusiasm, ready for the journey and anticipating what will come from the experience of putting together a book on UCAS personal statements. I can't help but think about the many meetings and opportunities to further refine university application strategies. At the moment, typing this preface with Jazz FM radio on in the background, I am currently imagining the enjoyable future experience of potentially having lunch with the person who leads undergraduate admissions at University College London (UCL) in a nice restaurant of an established London hotel and interviewing her about how UCL assesses their personal statements and the impact that this has on application success. (People who know me will understand . . . I like nice hotels). In between Googling the UCL admissions lead, I am now unavoidably finding myself looking up the composer of the Jazz FM piece that's currently playing – Chris Botti's take on 'My Funny Valentine' – very good!

It is currently the end of October. A lot has happened this month: I've not only had my 30th birthday, but I have also worked with a range of students to submit what I would define as extremely high-quality UCAS applications. UCAS has two main deadlines – the first falls in October (the early deadline), and the second (what's known as the 'equal consideration' deadline) typically falls in January. October is the date for those applying to Oxford, Cambridge, Medicine, Dentistry or Veterinary Science. January is for all other applicants. However, UCAS itself opens for submissions in September, and no matter which subjects or universities students choose, my personal strategy is to encourage all students to submit their applications by the end of September (aiming for before the early deadline). Doing so makes you come across to universities as extremely organised, motivated and, to some extent, gives you the first opportunity to be chosen. It also means that you get the UCAS application out of the way sooner and thus enabling more undivided time to focus on your current studies to get the best possible grades. Having enacted this process with the students I work with, as of today, I can confirm that the vast majority of students this year are already holding at least one conditional offer from a Russell Group university (even though the actual deadline isn't until next January). This, I am really happy about, and part of the success is down to the personal statement.

I have worked at four very different schools. Two of which can be described as rather elitist in terms of UK university ambitions – such as predominantly aiming for the coveted universities fitting under the terms of 'Oxbridge', 'G5' and the wider 'Russell Group'. Both schools (Oxford International College and Cardiff Sixth Form College), over the last few years, have been ranked as number one in the UK for A level results. So, I do appreciate that academic performance is also an important factor when it comes to university application success. Calibrate your choices based on your previously achieved (GCSE or equivalent) and current predicted grades. However, no matter the university, having an outstanding personal statement makes all the difference.

The seed of the idea of writing this book was planted several years ago, and as we have been getting closer and closer to the date when the changes to the UCAS personal statement format are being rolled out (2026 entry), I have found fewer and fewer reasons to delay its writing! Looking for a new challenge, I joined Cambridge's new branch of Cardiff Sixth Form College, two months ago, as their founding Head of Careers and Higher Education. Now that we have submitted our UCAS applications and I have started to fully settle into the flat (having built the desk and chair earlier today), I am looking forward to spending some evenings finalising this book for you.

Earlier today, I was put in contact with UCL's undergraduate admissions lead and I will be reaching out to set up meetings with G5 and RG institutions. I am keen to explore the updated changes to the personal statement and identify the ways in which highly competitive universities use these to assess students.

Therefore, such information will increase your chances of meeting these requirements. I'll be drawing upon my experiences of working with now what must be over one thousand students (in schools and my private consulting) to produce the highest-quality personal statements. In addition, I will be composing one of the few publications to first analyse and reflect on the new UCAS personal statement format. Thank you, in advance, for reading. Whether you are an aspiring student, family member of a student, or a professional member of staff, I wish you all the very best.

Dominic Fuge
31 October 2024
Cambridge, England

1 Introduction and background

It really is about making it attention-grabbing (and how to use this book)

The subtitle of this book, 'Create an attention-grabbing personal statement that gets noticed', is extremely intentional. The personal statement, from the outset, should make the admissions tutor recognise that the applicant is truly passionate, academically curious and is ultimately a good fit for their institution. Putting your personal spin on your UCAS personal statement is really important and certainly the number one way to help separate yourself from the competition – the competition being other applicants who are applying to the same university courses as you! When you apply to universities, as you can see in Figure 1 (overleaf), there are many ways in which applicants could be assessed by the admissions tutor, and much of these are quantitative data (e.g. their predicted grades).

Certainly, in numerical terms, there is not that much which could separate one candidate from another. To give you an example, in August 2024, the Office of Qualifications and Examinations Regulation (Ofqual) published data on A levels. If we take England alone, 188,875 students (66.8%) all took three subjects at A level and 76% of students in England, in 2024, obtained a C grade and above. Absolutely, taking more A levels or achieving exceptional results can help. For example, looking back at the same Ofqual data, only 4,135 students achieved three or more A*s (and hopefully the predicted grades submitted to UCAS more or less accurately reflected this!). However, generally speaking, there are a lot of applicants often with similar academic profiles and therefore the UCAS personal statement is the unique opportunity for students to add their individuality into the mix for admissions tutors to learn more about them. One of the key components of your strategy, for obtaining a place at

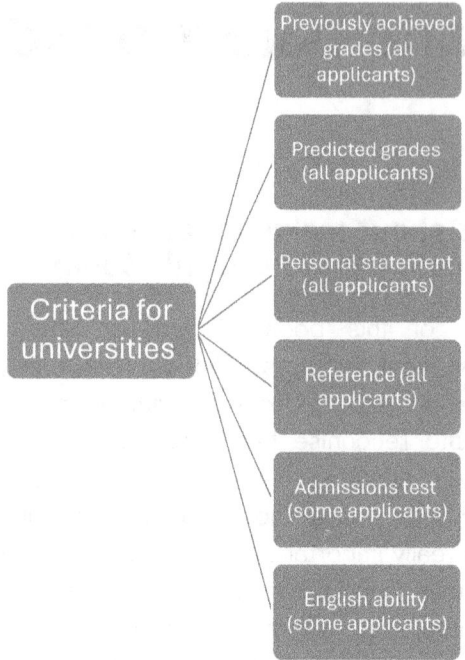

FIGURE 1: An overview of the main criteria UK universities use to assess undergraduate applications before making an interview offer/conditional offer. Listed in no particular order.

your preferred UK university, has to be to have an outstanding personal statement that grabs the attention of the reader.

Some admissions data to highlight the importance of personal statements

There are lots of personal statements out there, each year. Think about how many applications admissions tutors at universities have to assess. To give you an example of this, in 2022, the University of Bristol's Law School (a Russel Group institution currently ranked eighth for Law, in the Complete University Guide's 2025 league table) offered 1,255 places out of 3,235 undergraduate applicants. That's a considerable amount of personal statements for a department to go through. Imperial College London's Department of Aeronautics, in 2023, received 1,304 applications and made offers to only 299 of those. For another example, looking at a specific University of Oxford college, there were 1,278 candidates for 121 offers of places for Magdalen College's 2025 entry. Worldwide, as published in a

1 Introduction and Background

TABLE 1: Number of UCAS applicants in a 20-year sample, a steady increase.

Year	Applicants	Accepted applicants	Percentage (%) of successful applicants
2003	476,000	374,000	78.57
2004	486,000	378,000	77.77
2005	522,000	405,000	86.20
2006	506,000	391,000	77.27
2007	534,000	413,000	77.34
2008	589,000	457,000	77.59
2009	640,000	482,000	75.31
2010	697,000	487,000	69.87
2011	700,000	492,000	70.29
2012	654,000	465,000	71.10
2013	677,000	496,000	73.26
2014	700,000	512,000	73.14
2015	718,000	532,000	74.09
2016	718,000	535,000	74.51
2017	700,000	534,000	76.29
2018	696,000	533,000	76.58
2019	706,000	541,000	76.63
2020	729,000	570,000	78.19
2021	750,000	562,000	74.93
2022	767,000	563,000	73.40
2023	757,000	554,000	73.18

Source: Adapted from Bolton's (2024, p.8) 'Higher education student numbers', Commons Library Research Briefing.

document from the House of Commons Library, a total of 757,000 applicants for full-time undergraduate courses went through UCAS in 2023. As seen in Table 1, this number of applicants has been rising steadily throughout the years. UCAS, as expressed many times on their website and at their annual conferences over the last few years, which I have attended in person, predict that we'll reach a million higher education applicants per year from 2030. They are on what they call their 'journey to a million'. Therefore, for such coveted places at universities, while demand still outstrips supply in many circumstances, personal statements continue to be immensely important.

Moreover, for this current application cycle, at the time of writing, already, in the space of one month, 73,720 applicants submitted by the early deadline of 15 October 2024 (completed UCAS undergraduate applications could only be sent from 3 September 2024). A total of 600,660 applicants applied by the Equal Consideration Deadline of January 2025. The take-home message, I would say, is that there are a lot of personal statements out there, each year. End readers of these personal statements (university admissions tutors) need to be excited and inspired by what they read before they make the choice to ultimately positively assess your document and move it over to the successful pile. The UCAS personal statement is an important part of an applicant's profile and since so many are being submitted, to grab the attention of the reader, it needs to be captivating and effective. I would argue the best way to do this is to make it unique – avoid common clichés – and thus put the personal into personal statement. See Figure 2 for examples of common clichés to avoid and see Table 2 (overleaf) for a general timeline of relevant dates for the UCAS application process.

Using personal anecdotes to connect with the reader

Often, I am asked by students for techniques on how they can connect with the reader. Having spoken with and interviewed, formally and informally, lots of universities over the years (and many specifically for this book), I do think that personal anecdotes are a fantastic way to be unique and memorable. Not that long ago, for example, I was working with a student who wanted to apply to study Medicine. She gave an interesting example of walking down the street, and unfortunately, an elderly man collapsed outside of his home. She went over to help and later was informed that he unfortunately experienced a stroke. This then led her on a journey of wanting to learn more about this serious condition and medical emergency – whether it be through reading, attending guest lectures, participating in essay competitions or watching documentaries. This specific experience in her life, of witnessing a stroke, further cemented and catalysed the applicant's desire to undertake Medicine at university. This is an example of a personal story. The student used this story to highlight her academic curiosity by taking the experience and making it a platform to build academically relevant activities outside of the classroom (known as super-curricular activities). We'll talk a

1 Introduction and Background

FIGURE 2: Common clichés to avoid in your personal statement writing.

'I have always been interested in...'

'Since a young age...'

'From when I can first remember...'

→ A very common way to start. When using a blanket term covering the time of your whole existence (e.g. from when you can first remember) this comes across as vague, even if true, and therefore limits your opportunity to provide a specific moment for when you actually did cement your subject passion for the course you're applying to. Always, to be memorable and unique, open instead with specific personal anecdotes. Tell the story and connect with the reader. Avoid any sweeping and generic statements.

→ Quotations from books/films/podcasts, etc. are extremely overused. Especially when placed within an introductory paragraph. Where possible, avoid using quotations as not only are they very common but it can give the impression that you are using these to soak up space as you may have less words of your own to use. Instead, you can interpret something you've read but explain the content and significance in your own words. If you are hoping to use a quote, shorter and concise ones, on the whole, are more effective.

'As said by...'

'A quote from...'

'As written in...'

'I found this very interesting...'

→ If said on its own, that you found something interesting, as a statement without going a lot deeper, this is meaningless. To highlight your subject passion and knowledge, amplify your depth of understanding by using key terminology and technical insight to reflect on the topic/theory/experience etc. you are referring to. Be specific and show your understanding by engaging with the subject

→ Ultimately, you are making a sales pitch to the university. Why should they gravitate towards you rather than making an offer to another candidate? Thus, you should be bold and proud of your achievements, as opposed to possibly risking coming across as unenthusiastic or shy due to being self-deprecating or overly humble. Market yourself and show your strengths. Certainly, however, you can use setbacks to show your character and growth (if relevant). But this can be a risky strategy and more often than not best to avoid.

'I am relatively proficient at...'

'I have taken part in a lot of extracurriculars...'

'As I have read in numerous books...'

→ Certainly, as we'll see later in this book, you do need a lot of extra activities. Nevertheless, avoid simply listing what you've done or gloss over experiences without being very specific – e.g. what did you learn, what did you enjoy and how has this cemented your desire to study this course at university? Also, there is a difference between the terms 'extra-curricular' and 'super-curricular', as we'll explore in this book.

TABLE 2: A timeline for UCAS applications.

Month	Before or on year of entry	Deadline/event	Explanation
April	Before	UCAS course choice search tool opens	You can now view which university courses are available for the next application cycle
May	Before	UCAS registration opens for the following year's entry	It is now possible to create an account and start applications in the UCAS Hub
September	Before	Applications can now be submitted	Once fully complete, UCAS applications can be submitted after this date
October	Before	Early October Deadline	Deadline for specific courses (Oxbridge & majority of Medicine; Dentistry; Veterinary Science) for equal consideration
January	On	Equal Consideration Deadline	The deadline for an equal consideration for the majority of all undergraduate courses
February	On	UCAS Extra opens	For those who are not holding any offers and have used all five choices can apply for an additional course that is still available
June	On	Final opportunity to add an Extra choice	The last chance applicants have to add an additional course choice should they be eligible
July	On	Clearing opens	Courses that have unfilled places (e.g. due to applicants not meeting the conditions of their offer) are displayed and all applicants have the chance to apply to these

Note: Specific dates within the month have been omitted as these can, on occasion, vary each year. Do check the UCAS website for up-to-date dates and information.

lot more about super-curricular activities and how to build your profile later in this book. From all of the personal statements I have read and worked through with students, when it comes to sincere personal stories and unique experiences, I have rarely (if ever!) seen the same examples. I am not entirely sure how, but for some reason, there are so many personal journeys for how students find their subject passion, even for the same degree. If you are a student, reflect on this and I am confident that your personal stories will come if they are not already known to you!

Resources you can use

Throughout this book, you will find figures and tables that have hints and tips, as well as interesting information. **Pages ix–x** have a list to show you where all these can be found, should you ever want to source a specific figure or table. This book is cumulative, developing your UCAS personal statement planning and writing. Therefore, I would recommend, especially for future university applicants as opposed to school career advisers and university guidance counsellors, that you read through this in the correct sequence from page to page. Having said this, you are all very busy individuals, and so there may be times when you would like to skim through/dip in and out. See the contents page to point you in the right direction. The UCAS personal statement has a framework of three specific questions. In Chapter 4 of this book, there is a specific subsection devoted to each question. Some figures and tables are actually template resources, designed for students to write in (worksheets). Worksheets and other resources can be downloaded from the Trotman website (see the QR code at the front of this book). Again, see the list of figures and tables to know on which pages these can be found. All the information, advice and guidance presented here is of my own choosing and so may differ from others and so please do keep this in mind. Consult with others, too, before finalising your university choices and submitting your personal statement.

Why UCAS has changed the personal statement format (and does it matter?)

Certainly this change to the UCAS personal statement format, from initially having a 4,000-character free-text field to now (for 2026 entry), having three set questions, has ignited debate among those in higher education. (Debate both publicly and confidentially behind the scenes.) If you ask UCAS directly why they have modified the long-standing format, they will tell you that this is due to levelling the playing field. In a 4,000-character (including spaces) personal statement without a prescribed structure, the style among students varied immensely. In fact, I saw this from many candidates. When working in schools, as I do now, or as a private consultant, I would often ask students to first produce a plan or even attempt a first draft. Some students would do an excellent job – such as by engaging the reader with an interesting introductory paragraph containing an anecdote about the reasons for wanting to take on this degree at university – while other students would need far more guidance. For example, their first paragraph would look more like a conclusion or the main body. By removing the ambiguity and student autonomy to fully design the shape of their free text, UCAS can level the playing field for students who do not have access to guidance from a careers and higher education counsellor such as myself. For instance, perhaps they are studying at a school without access to a careers professional, or the student comes from a family where they are the first to go to university and therefore may not have access to the same firsthand knowledge.

UCAS references have already changed (in a similar way to the personal statements)

In fact, changing a 4,000-character free-text format to three questions is absolutely not unique. UCAS has already done exactly the same to their references. When students apply to university through UCAS, they will need a personal statement that they write and also a reference written by their school (or nominated individual if they are applying independently). For the last two years of application cycles, instead of giving schools the ability to write freely, UCAS has adopted the framework of three specific sections. The first is a section about the school; the second is to outline any mitigating circumstances or medical issues (sometimes left blank); the third is the most substantial part where the referee will write about the applicant's suitability for the university course. Some schools were very good at structuring an interesting and useful reference for their students, in the old free-text version, while others were not. The three questions attempted to try and standardise the information and value coming from the reference. Therefore, we have seen this change before and have been expecting modifications to come to the personal statement as well as the reference. Changing both the reference and personal statement may have been too much in one go and so it has been staggered.

UCAS going through an admissions reform

The idea of UCAS wanting to level the playing field has existed for some time. It was in their 'Future of Undergraduate Admissions' report, published at the start of 2023, where they discussed concepts relating to admission reform. For instance, they have removed the UCAS application fee (last year being £28.50 for all five UCAS choices) for students eligible for free school meals. The objective of changing expectations and widening participation can be a contentious topic. On the one hand, some may describe this as noble and worthwhile and on the other side of the spectrum it can be seen as an unreasonable or unnecessary lowering of expectations.

Whether we see this new personal statement modification as just or unjust, it ultimately does not matter. The reason I say this is because all of the essential content that I have been coaching for the best part of a decade still remains untouched. In addition, the vast majority of the work is not actually the writing but it's the going out and participating in relevant subject exploration activities (which then gives you the material to write about). Furthermore, it is still going to be your personal style and approach when answering the three personal statement questions which will set your application apart from others. Whether I was publishing this book several years ago or today, much of the book's information, advice and guidance will have remained unchanged.

An example of the 'old' personal statement

To illustrate the above point, I wanted to share with you a recent example of a UCAS personal statement submitted by a student I worked with for the 2025 entry cycle, at Cardiff Sixth Form College, Cambridge. This personal statement is the last example of what was the original 4,000-character free-text versions without the three set questions. There are two reasons why I selected this particular personal statement as the example to use in this chapter. Firstly, it is because the student kindly volunteered to share his personal statement knowing that I was publishing a book. Secondly, for those teachers, careers advisers and university counsellors reading this book, I know that you will appreciate the particular structure of this original 4,000-character piece. It is a very classic and 'textbook', if you will, common example of a simple and effective style. As we prepare to write (or provide guidance) on the new personal statement format, why not look at a very typical example of the previous style to know how to build out. The applicant who wrote this personal statement did very well in receiving offers from the University of Bath; University of Edinburgh; University of Exeter; Loughborough University. See the personal statement, for Mechanical Engineering, below. I have then written a commentary underneath – providing some reflection and critique on this piece plus also some suggestions of what we can extrapolate from this example when starting to prepare for the new personal statements.

Personal statement example ('old' version)

At the age of 8 years, I built a thermometer using an Arduino microcontroller, thermostats, and YouTube videos. At the age of 10, I created a solar-powered car model. At school, when I noticed a plant wilting, I was motivated to develop an automated soil moisture-based watering system to save it. From a young age, I have had a passion for innovation and problem-solving in sustainability, motivating me to study mechanical engineering so that I can positively impact the environment.

After reading 'In Search of Schrödinger's Cat' (Gribbin, 1984), I was struck by scientists' willingness to take risks and embrace failures in their pursuit of knowledge. This reinforced my understanding of perseverance in engineering and solidified my commitment to contributing to sustainable technological advancements in the future. This motivated me to focus my Extended Project Qualification on superconductors to create something renewable with a positive global impact. Embracing the challenges of this project, I built an Arduino-Controlled Superconductor Maglev Train, tackling obstacles such as shaping the magnetic track, and acquiring liquid nitrogen. Ultimately, I developed a functional prototype that demonstrated the potential of superconductors for sustainable transportation.

Seeking real-world experience, I interned at Vitol Electric Vehicle, where I analysed optimal locations for electric vehicle chargers, considering factors such as parking and pedestrian access. This role emphasized that engineering extends beyond hands-on work; it involves evaluating design practicality and understanding end-user interactions. This internship underscored the importance of critical thinking and analytical skills in engineering, particularly in optimizing designs for practical applications.

Recognizing the collaborative nature of engineering, I participated in the Rutherford Appleton Laboratory Space Project, where I worked with five other students to design a model sounding rocket capable of carrying a 500 g payload and achieving 50 m/s² acceleration at launch. I selected materials that balanced strength, weight, and cost, such as basswood for the fins and balsa wood for the nose cone. I also attended a summer event at The Engineering & Design Institute. We were divided into groups of four and were tasked with creating an efficient windmill using cardboard, sticks, tape, and paper. Utilising my A level understanding of torque and aerodynamics, we completed the windmill on time and won an award for the most efficient windmill. These projects enhanced my teamwork skills as we tackled challenges and supported one another.

Understanding that mechanical engineering demands a strong foundation in both physics and mathematics, I participated in the UK senior Maths and Physics challenges, earning a bronze and a silver respectively. Alongside four other students, I ranked in the top 20 percent internationally in the MathWorks Math Modelling Challenge. I earned a distinction in the UK Bebras Challenge and reached the finals of the Northeastern University London Essay Competition.

As president of my school's Engineering, Football, and Volleyball clubs, and an active member of Basketball and Model UN clubs, I developed key skills such as leadership, teamwork, and problem-solving, crucial for a successful career in mechanical engineering. Beyond school, I engage in recycling projects, which foster creativity and innovative thinking, and I mentor GCSE students in Maths, enhancing my ability to explain concepts from different perspectives and improving my communication skills.

I am confident that a degree in mechanical engineering will allow me to build on these experiences and contribute to creating larger-scale projects that promote sustainability and innovation, similar to the impactful work done by companies like Tesla and Siemens AG. My goal is to become a successful mechanical engineer, dedicated to making the Earth a greener and more sustainable place.

Commentary on this personal statement

By typical example of the style, what I mean is that we have a very clear overall structure – an introduction, main body and conclusion. This used to be the standard guidance for good personal statement structure with the 4,000-character free text. The introduction offers a personal anecdote and view into the applicant's mind resulting in his ultimate choice to select Mechanical Engineering for university study. In the words of the applicant, he has been on a journey of wanting to innovate from a young age. His passion for creating things, compounded by his interest in sustainability, offered the crystallising moment of realising that Mechanical Engineering is the best-fit choice for his future studies.

In the main body, we see a good selection of super-curricular activities further highlighting his passion for the university course. What I also thought was particularly effective in this personal statement was the theme/thread maintained between the introduction and conclusion – an excitement for innovative sustainable solutions in engineering. While there possibly could have been some more subject-specific content regarding the science behind relevant engineering topics – for example, on the superconductors or design of a model sounding rocket – there were some moments of good reflection on what was learned or enjoyed during some of these experiences – thus reinforcing the academic curiosity and passion for the course. When producing a personal statement, perhaps due to the character count or time constraints, there will often be thoughts about what could have been added or changed. Nonetheless, the key is to work with what you have to produce a piece that has been refined over many drafts (with teacher, family or peer feedback) that ultimately reads well, has a good number of super-curricular activities and that you are finally happy with.

As we move towards the end of the main body, there is a penultimate paragraph containing the non-academic (known as extra-curricular) material. The majority of this personal statement was academic, however, to display an overall roundedness of personal skills and qualities, there was a sprinkle towards the end of things outside of academia. In this case, the applicant referred to some sports and community volunteering.

Turning to the 'new' (current) personal statement

When looking to the new personal statement, I think this older version, from last year's application cycle, offers us a flavour of the essential ingredients. We still need an engaging introduction with the crystallising moment for why this university course was selected; a main body containing a good number of relevant super-curricular experiences; a sprinkle of non-academic activities to showcase roundedness; a conclusion to further highlight to the reader that this university course, out of the plethora of other options that may be available, is the right choice. The new three-question-format personal statement does also possess these ingredients, albeit with now subheadings. Question 1 will contain the introductory paragraph and majority of super-curricular content; Question 2 will have some more super-curricular content but the focus will be on classroom subjects (this is new); Question 3 will be the sprinkle of non-academic (extra-curricular).

There are six examples, found in Chapter 7 of this book, of the new UCAS personal statement (or what now could also be called 'usual'). I have also written commentaries underneath each one.

The higher education landscape of UK universities

Going to university is a significant life decision. It is a huge investment of time, money and other resources. Choosing the pursuit of higher education studies, in some ways, closes or delays other paths that one could take. Namely, starting full-time employment and earning a salary! To many, including my younger self, taking the leap of joining a university was a rite of passage and a sensible buffer between secondary school and the world of work. I didn't have a clear sense of what career I wanted to pursue. Being inspired by evolutionary biology and ancient civilisations, I went on to complete a degree in Archaeology and Anthropology, at Durham University. While I did get to spend a month excavating in a Bronze Age cave of Southern Italy, after several experiences of digging in the pouring rain of Northern England, I soon realised that opportunities to emulate an Indiana Jones lifestyle may be less numerous than I previously thought. I did not fully choose university, if I am reflecting back, exclusively with employment in mind. I went, certainly, to have a degree which enhances my chances of securing a job (whatever that job may end up being) but also for the intellectual enrichment and self-development that university study provides. I selected Durham, as I was looking for somewhere with a historic tradition, a collegiate environment and for a new challenge having grown up in London as an only child. The Northeast is pretty different to London. At university, I made friends, took part in activities (e.g. being president of the Archaeology Society, learning about business through the Blueprint Enterprise Programme and pursuing my hobby of clay pigeon shooting, to name but a few experiences). I learned a lot about myself and also used university as a platform to develop skills for life. I actually liked university to the point where I later went on to study two postgraduate qualifications, at the University of Edinburgh and then University of Cambridge. When considering the UK higher education landscape, don't just think about the university course but try to explore what you want the return on investment to be, and this should help you help yourself in joining an institution where you will thrive.

Considering whether university is right for you

As government figures continuously show, completing an undergraduate degree is beneficial. For example, increasing your chances of employment and earning larger salaries. When Googling the reasons for going to university, as you might expect, there are lots of articles appearing, written by universities, to highlight why you should become an undergraduate student (and specifically join them!) – whether it be research opportunities and academic excellence; networking and lifelong friends; use of impressive facilities; experiencing mentorship; developing employability skills. The UK is synonymous with high quality and reputation when it comes to universities. Higher education in the UK is a big driver of economic growth, social mobility and representing the UK's image across the globe. Therefore, the UK government is understandably protective of this service. This is indicated by the recent decision (the first time in eight years) to increase the maximum fees for standard full-time university courses for UK students (rising by 3.1% to £9,535 from 1st August 2025). Fees for international students have consistently been higher without an equal cap, sometimes being twice, three or even close to four times the price of those with a home fee status. So, again, do consider whether university is right for you. I would argue that it is an amazing choice – an exciting and enriching experience awaits. However, you have to be sure and certainly one size does not fit all.

How many universities are there and how to choose between them?

When building a university shortlist – selecting your preferred subject area and ultimate list of five universities for UCAS – it naturally would be useful for you to first know what's on the table. How many universities are there and what are some useful trends/statistics/snippets of information that you can draw upon to make considered and effective choices? To have degree awarding powers and to use the 'university' title is something protected by law. Therefore, when you see this title you can rest assured that there is a certain baseline of acceptable quality. In addition to university rankings, league tables and university groups (more of this in Chapter 2 of the book), the main metrics that I use to judge how many universities there are and what's available in the UK (and thus going back to what's on the table for students) is to look at two lists. The first is known as Universities UK (UUK) and the second is to read the annual publication, named *The Times and Sunday Times Good University Guide* (usually published every February). The UUK is a registered charity, with vice-chancellors and principals of UK universities as members. They work together as an advisory organisation. Due to the nature of this organisation, one can assume that the majority of UK universities ought to really be members of this and at the time of double checking (April 2025) I can see that there are 141 member universities. *The Times and Sunday Times Good University Guide* has a very useful one-page breakdown of each university, towards the back of the book, in its 'University Profiles' chapter. There are 134 universities profiled in the 2026 Guide (published in February 2025). So, to give a round figure, we can say that there are around 150 institutions to choose from.

What is also noticeable about *The Times and Sunday Times Good University Guide* is that, each year, they give out a series of awards for particular accolades. For example, 'University of the Year for Student Experience', 'Specialist University of the Year' and 'Modern University of the Year'. This is a great way to learn more about what's available as well as the ways in which universities could be assessed. They also have an overall league table and this year, in the 2026 rankings, for the first time in the 31-year history of *The Times and Sunday Times Good University Guide*, the London School of Economics and Political Science (LSE) has taken the coveted award of being first place number one university in the UK. Last year's winner, as well as this year's runner up, is the University of St Andrew's. Third place went to the University of Oxford, fourth was the University of Cambridge and fifth place went to Durham University. Interestingly, *The Times and Sunday Times Good University Guide* has subject-specific guides and rankings. Students may come across subject areas that they are less familiar with but later realise that this could be a potential option to pursue or at least learn more about. This list of subject areas is extensive – from Food Science to Celtic Studies. Rankings are not necessarily everything and the importance one places on rankings and awards varies from individual to individual. Naturally, there are many other criteria that one may have to find their best-fit institution and university course. Nevertheless, league tables and subject-specific rankings do help to provide an overview of what is available in the UK, including which university departments excel in particular areas, and so I would encourage you to explore these.

Linking the personal statement to the same subject area

What is also notable about UK universities, bringing it back to personal statements, is that the subject area you choose (e.g. Biochemistry, Radiography, etc.) is what you will be studying from the very start. Each year will be made up of modules/papers and you'll have some which are mandatory and others which are optional and you can build your own programme. The vast majority of modules/papers will come from the subject area you've applied to. You may have an opportunity to add one external module/paper but this will only be a very small portion of your degree. This approach to undergraduate university study differs from some other models, such as in the United States, which is known for offering a broad range of subjects where students later specialise with majors and minors (a liberal arts style). (Note that Liberal Arts, while less common and structured slightly differently to the US, can also be taken in the UK.) This singularly of university course specialisation is why UCAS require a personal statement that all five universities will see. This personal statement is specific to your selection of the university course (subject area) and so involves a lot of content which highlights your subject passion, academic curiosity and suitability for the university course, as opposed to being more down the lines of creative writing that you might find in other countries.

2 Finding your right course

Vocational vs. subject passion

A very common question you'll return to time and time again, and something often presented to careers professionals such as myself, is the question of how to choose the right course at university. In ultimately the majority, if not all books, articles, podcasts, talks and webinars about choosing a course, the answer will inevitably be the same. The distinctively common answer being: 'Only you can answer this question.' In some ways, as the recipient of this possibly blunt answer, future applicants may well be slightly frustrated and confused as to how reaching out for advice and guidance has only resulted in the decision being boomeranged back to them! In some ways, I agree with those who say that the choice is yours, but I also feel that often college counsellors, heads of careers (and similar job titles) fall short of giving students the full answer. Yes, you do choose, but I think university applicants should be armed with useful parameters and frameworks to best make the right decision. The first step, in my opinion, is to consider whether your career and university aim is what's known as 'vocational' or what I would call 'subject passion'.

After all, as you will most likely be aware by this point, you only have one personal statement that can be submitted alongside your UCAS application. You can choose up to five universities to apply to (see Figure 3 for the university choice caveats – there are some nuances that alter the flexibility of your five choices), and so students must be confident about their university subject choice. This is because all five university choices will see the exact same personal statement and, therefore, to be as effective as possible, it is best that this personal statement tackles a single subject area rather than dividing your personal statement into different subject choices as you are applying to

2 Finding Your Right Course

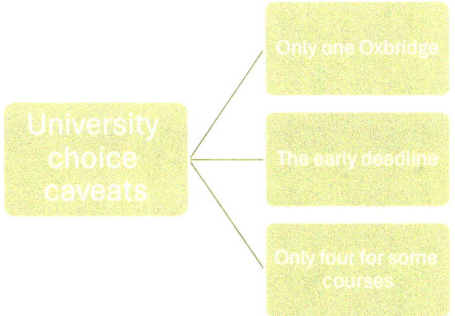

FIGURE 3: University choice caveats to consider when making your selection of five courses. Listed in no particular order.

different course choices. Doing so wouldn't be advantageous at all, as if applicants are mentioning a course in their personal statement which they haven't selected for a university reading this, it'll make them come across as possibly dispassionate and unprepared. Select five university courses which are similar and then write a single personal statement that is very much tailored to all of these choices. Identifying which courses you would like to study is the first step of writing your UCAS personal statement. The second step, which is Chapter 3 of this book, is to engage in super-curricular profile-building specific for your chosen courses.

So, going back to 'vocational' and 'subject passion', there are two main ways to identify a university course. Consider whether you have a specific career goal in mind or whether you are simply driven by a strong academic interest in a particular subject area. For the former, following a specific career goal ('vocational'), you are choosing a course to launch into a career. As an example, if you would like to become an architect, you'll need to study Architecture; if you desire to become an engineer, you'll require an Engineering degree; if you would like to be a medic, you'll need to study Medicine; being a lawyer requires a law degree. You get the idea! On the other hand, you might be interested in a subject area but not have a career in mind. From my experience working with sixth-form-aged students, many will change their ideas about which career is right for them. This organic process of mind changing is normal and beneficial as you search for your best fit. Do as much research as possible – speak with friends, family, teachers and, if possible, go on work experience for a few days and/or watch some vlogs about the life of someone in a particular career or subject area. A common anecdote that I use often is the example of a student I worked with a few years ago. She was very curious about law and did several interesting activities and eventually secured work experience with a local law firm for a week. She left the work experience being really uninspired about legal practice – noting the amount of dense document reading, fine attention to written detail and a feeling of partaking in (her opinion, of course!) menial tasks. This was roughly one year before the university application deadline. After more digging, she realised that Law was not her right fit, and she later went on to study Medicine at the University of Cambridge! It's natural to change your mind – explore, engage, evaluate and then be effective in pursuing your chosen course after you've exhausted the research process and satisfied your own reasons for wanting to choose a subject area.

Subject passion is perhaps the most stable

To further illustrate that career preferences can change, a peer-reviewed paper published by Quinlan and Corbin (2023) identified, from a survey of 663 students based at a mid-ranked UK university, 61% reported that their career aspirations had changed during their time at university. Therefore, I think what's often more stable is the passion one has for a subject area as opposed to the idea of the job at the end of the academic journey tunnel. Remember, you will be studying this for at least three years, and if you enjoy what you're doing, you'll find the hard work immeasurably easier. You may not want to be a historian as a future job, but you are excited about the subject of history; working as a professional politician might not be right for you, but you would be fascinated to have the opportunity to learn more about this at university; you may only see yourself travelling to exotic places for pleasure rather than work, but would gravitate towards a geography degree. Again, you can see this division of choosing something because you need this for a particular career or selecting a degree because you happen to have a deep subject passion.

2 Finding Your Right Course

Already, you have probably identified that the choice of vocational or subject passion is not mutually exclusive. For instance, you could want to be an engineer (vocational) but then also have a deep academic curiosity (subject passion) for engineering. If you have a specific career in mind and you are motivated enough to follow this into university, that is fantastic. Equally, if you don't have a specific career in mind but have a subject area you are excited by and are considering exploring further at university, this is also fantastic. I have devised a matrix (Table 3) to help students consider finding their right university course. Table 4 has a list of degree subject examples, divided by vocational and

TABLE 3: Vocational vs. Subject Passion Matrix. Identify whether the course/subject area you are considering for undergraduate study at university is vocational and/or a subject interest. As the matrix indicates, to be a potentially good fit option, it must be a subject passion but does not necessarily have to be vocational.

Vocational	Subject passion	A potential good fit course for university study
✓	✓	Yes
✓	X	No
X	✓	Yes
X	X	No

TABLE 4: Examples of some 'vocational' and 'subject passion' university course choices. In alphabetical order.

Examples of some university courses divided into two categories	
Vocational	Subject passion
Architecture	Archaeology
Dentistry	Business
Engineering	Classics
Law	Economics
Medicine	English Literature
Pharmacy	Geography
Psychology	History
Veterinary Science	Philosophy

Note: This is not a fully exhaustive list and these two categories are not mutually exclusive.

subject passion. Again, not mutually exclusive but gives you a good idea.

Choosing a degree for future success

In fact, the most popular question these days I receive from students and sometimes parents alike is not what to study but how this degree choice will impact future career opportunities. People, perhaps rightly so, seem to be driven by ultimate career fulfilment and success, and those applying to university may well be doing so because they see the university degree as an essential part of the process for later career growth. Well, the good news is that your future is not fully defined by what you study. A great example of this can be found in the concept of the 'squiggly career' – you can read more in a fantastic (and now very well-known) book with this same title, authored by Tupper and Ellis (2020). There are plenty of transferable skills that you can take with you to find a future job after university – whether you secure a graduate scheme, reconnect with a previous work experience provider or enter the job market through another means. Medics do sometimes go into business and become entrepreneurs; slightly over half of lawyers in the UK did not study Law for their undergraduate degree; I had a colleague who was a school Deputy Head and managed pastoral matters and the boarding house – he studied Sports Science! Your degree does not always dictate your future career path. What actually has a greater influence on your career trajectory, in my opinion, is that you have settled into a high-quality university and are motivated enough by what you're studying that you end up securing a decent grade at the end of your degree. It's also important to have fun at university and participate in wider university life – network with companies and add to your CV! The lens of vocational vs. subject passion may offer some focus to help students assess their current interests and future choices.

Ways to conduct research (and which types of degrees are available)

In the same way as we just divided the criteria of 'vocational' and 'subject passion', I think there is also a binary viewpoint when conducting university research – finding a course that truly captivates you. These are 'specific university' and 'specific course'. Again, these are not necessarily mutually exclusive, but dividing these perspectives offers us a way to consider how one may go about conducting their research and then ultimately finding their best-fit institution and university degree. By specific university, what I mean is that some students are motivated by securing a place at specific universities. Perhaps, this university is narrowed by ranking (e.g. ranked top 10 for a particular subject), is part of a recognised prestigious group (e.g. G5 or the Russell Group), or is based in a preferred part of the UK. Moreover, students may have other criteria that they would prefer to have from the university irrespective of the course (e.g. a vibrant nightlight, a historical city centre or a popular café culture). Figure 4 contains a bullet point list of some preferences that students may have when researching institutions irrespective of the course offered.

FIGURE 4: Preferences that students may have when selecting their universities. Bullets listed in alphabetical order.

- Accommodation (e.g. types offered and availability)
- Affordability
- Cultural aspects (both of the university and wider area)
- Distance from family and friends
- Facilities overall (e.g. gyms and libraries)
- Geographic location
- Links with employers and offerings from the careers service
- Nightlife
- Notable alumni
- Pre-existing links with the university (e.g. family and friends who have attended)
- Publishing of interesting research
- Ranking and reputation
- Size of the town or city
- Specific clubs and societies offered
- Whether more traditional or modern in feel
- Whether there is a large campus or the university is spread throughout a city

Prestigious university groups

The vast majority of countries who have a large number of universities tend to have specific prestigious groups of institutions. For example, the 'Ivy League' in the US; 'SKY' universities in South Korea; 'Group of Eight' (Go8) in Australia; the 'League of European Research Universities' (LERU). These groups are mostly associated with cutting-edge research, high ranking and thus competitive admissions. Famously, not all of these universities were initially grouped based exclusively on

TABLE 5: The 27 UK universities, divided by prestigious group. (This includes the author's 'Universities to Consider' [U2C]).

University	Oxbridge	Stoxbridge	U2C	G5	LERU	Russell Group
Cardiff University						✓
Durham University						✓
Imperial College London				✓	✓	✓
King's College London						✓
London School of Economics				✓		✓
Loughborough University			✓			
Newcastle University						✓
Queen Mary, University of London						✓
Queen's University Belfast						✓
University College London				✓	✓	✓
University of Bath						
University of Birmingham						✓
University of Bristol						✓
University of Cambridge	✓	✓		✓	✓	✓

(*Continued*)

TABLE 5: (Continued)

University	Oxbridge	Stonebridge	G28	G5	LERU	Russell Group
University of Edinburgh					✓	✓
University of Exeter						✓
University of Glasgow						✓
University of Leeds						✓
University of Liverpool						✓
University of Manchester						✓
University of Nottingham						✓
University of Oxford	✓	✓		✓	✓	✓
University of Sheffield						✓
University of Southampton						✓
University of St Andrews		✓	✓			
University of Warwick						✓
University of York						✓

prestige – for instance, the eight institutions of the Ivy League initially stemmed from location in the United States, as well as sports membership. Nevertheless, over the years, especially, a shared history and global recognition has meant that these universities attract highly driven students and are respected by employers. The UK is no exception and has a few groups of its own – Oxbridge, G5 and the Russell Group. Table 5 shows you all these UK universities who are part of prestigious groups (27 universities in total). Rather egotistically, I must admit, I have also created my own group, known as 'Universities to Consider' (U2C). These are made up of three universities – the University of St Andrews, University of Bath and Loughborough University. The reason for putting these universities into a group is because they are extremely high ranking and leading in many ways, but are not part of the Russell Group. Lots of colleagues in the industry, other career advisers and university counsellors, have pondered on the reasons why these institutions are not part of the Russell Group. There have been a variety of theories and, having spoken with these institutions, my best reading between the lines is that not being part of the group might actually help their marketing (e.g. not dwarfed by being one of the many in the group), and also as they have leading but not always large academic departments, it sometimes may not be possible to fully keep up with particular research-intensive projects. They want to stand on their own. As mentioned, rankings can be particularly high – St Andrew's has consistently ranked as the number one best university in the UK, by The Guardian University Guide, over the last couple of years. This has, in the industry, created a new group, adding St Andrew's to 'Oxbridge' (Oxford and Cambridge), which is affectionately known as 'Stoxbridge'.

When it comes to deciding whether to include any of these prestigiously grouped universities as one of your five UCAS choices, this is, of course, very dependent on the student. For example, some students I have worked with are very motivated by securing a place at one of these institutions, and others are less concerned about these prestigious groups and are selecting universities based on other best-fit criteria. Moreover, these universities are competitive and therefore often (but not exclusively) have high entry requirements and so students should have high predicted grades. Entry requirements vary massively based on subjects and so check the entry requirements directly on the university website or other websites dedicated to university searches (see Table 6 overleaf for some suggested websites). When choosing university courses, perceived risk plays a big part. Some students are willing to take a gap year if they do not secure a place at their preferred institution, and others adopt a 'UCAS plus' model (i.e. applying to other universities around the world to diversify their portfolio). Therefore, they can be more risky as they have more options. Some students I have worked with have all five UCAS choices being part of the Russell Group, some have had just a few and others none at all. So, the decision is very student-focused. Some universities who are part of the prestigious groups do not offer specific courses that might be of interest to the student and so this is another reason why they may or may not include such institutions on their shortlist.

Types of university courses

Now, moving on to the second viewpoint, 'specific course', another way to research is to have a particular subject area in mind and see which universities offer these. For instance, a student may already have a definite subject area in mind. These could be single honours, one subject, such as Law, Mathematics or Psychology. These could also be joint honours, such as 'Archaeology and Anthropology', 'Economics and Finance' or 'Computing and Mathematics'. A note about joint honours: if there is an 'and' in the middle, such as 'Archaeology and Anthropology', then the course content is divided roughly equally between the subjects; when the word 'with' is used, such as 'Economics with Finance', then it is a major-minor-type split (e.g. 70:30). There are also combined honours and well-known subject clusters, perhaps none more famous than 'Philosophy, Politics and Economics' (PPE). If you have specific subjects in mind, then you could directly search for subject rankings and then identify which universities offer the particular course and then work your way through these until you find options that fit your personal preference criteria. As mentioned earlier, the lens of specific university vs. specific course is not mutually exclusive, but can offer a useful way to start the research and thus identify what's available.

TABLE 6: Some recommended websites for university research.

Name	Website	Overview
CUG	www.thecompleteuniversityguide.co.uk	This is a very user-friendly site, which is extremely well-known. Offers both subject and university-wide rankings; specific summaries about universities to help establish best fit; can search for courses based on predicted grades. A sidenote is that they do some great posters and do willingly send these to schools.
Discover Uni	www.discoveruni.gov.uk	A great resource to search for available university courses. Moreover, this site provides a tremendously broad range of useful data – e.g. average earnings for graduates from specific courses; student perceptions about the course after being surveyed.
Oxbridge Applications	www.oxbridgeapplications.com	Offers holistic application support and mentoring, specifically for candidates aiming for the University of Oxford or University of Cambridge. From admissions tests to interviews, there's a lot on offer.
The Lawyer Portal	www.thelawyerportal.com	This is specific for law applicants. They regularly update a useful page, for example, about LNAT – e.g. which universities are using this admissions test and how to prepare. They also have lots of general guidance about studying Law and higher education study.
The Medic Portal	www.themedicportal.com	This is specific for Medicine applicants. Similar to the Lawyer Portal, they have a comprehensive range of support and information. It's particularly useful to stay up to date with their guidance on UCAT and how universities use admission test scores – be strategic with your medical school choices!
The Student Room	www.thestudentroom.co.uk	This is a well-known forum for UK school and university students. Naturally, with such a big online community, you will have to keep in mind that many responses are very subjective – which perhaps is one of the benefits of this website. Balance these views with your own research.
UCAS	www.ucas.com	The UCAS website is not just a platform to submit university applications, but it also hosts a very useful range of information, advice and guidance. Highlights include the 'how-to'-style articles, university subject area pages and a careers quiz to help students find their best fit.
Uni Compare	www.universitycompare.com	Uni Compare allows you to explore specific courses and also helps students engage with universities. For example, you can download directly or request prospectuses with a click of the button. It also houses some very useful guides and displays open day dates.

When students start the search process, they often ask what the letters after the name of the university course mean. Degree abbreviations include (but are by no means limited to) BArch; BA; BBA; BEd; BMedSci; BSc; LLB. These are used to define an academic degree as opposed to spelling out the title in full. A 'BArch', for example, stands for 'Bachelor of Architecture' and 'LLB' stands for 'Bachelor of Laws'. Degree abbreviations are not always exclusive to a particular subject and the most common are BA and BSc. A 'BA' is 'Bachelor of Arts' and 'BSc' is 'Bachelor of Sciences'. BSc degrees are those that contain an element of Mathematics/Science within the course and historically these have been deemed, rightly or wrongly, as slightly more prestigious in the job market as opposed to a BA degree. This interpretation, in my opinion, has mostly come from parents and some employers but more often than not I would say that the abbreviation is less important than the specific university, final score, or what the student got out of the degree and how they use this to market themselves to employers when applying for jobs in the future. Therefore, whether it is a BA in Psychology, for instance, or a BSc in Psychology, look more closely at how the degree is structured and what modules are taught within the degree when deciding which courses make your final five for the UCAS application.

Creating your university shortlist

Creating your university shortlist is not just about knowing what's available but you should also be strategic. The ways in which students need to be strategic are dependent on the profile of the student (e.g. what they're studying at school and what their predicted grades will be) as well as the specific university course they're applying to. For courses that require additional admissions tests, such as Medicine, you should look at the admissions test cut-offs and how scores are interpreted by each institution. Some have lower cut-offs than others, or place specific focus on parts of the admissions test. Seasoned university counsellors would often advise that 'If you simply want to go to Cambridge, you should not choose Medicine'. What they mean by this is that if you have a degree in mind then you need to strategically choose the right university for your profile as opposed to blindly focusing on the institution. Indeed, there are courses less competitive than Medicine that are offered at Cambridge. By the way, this is not to say that prospective medics should not choose the University of Cambridge – indeed, I have seen many be admitted to Cambridge – it just means that you should only choose Cambridge as one of your UCAS choices if it is strategic.

Double checking entry requirements

When creating a shortlist, students first need to consider whether there are any admissions tests required and how can they select a range of universities that will increase their chances of receiving some offers. There are university courses of the same subject, in some examples, where only a few universities require an admissions test. Law is an example of this. For instance, only nine UK universities for Law require students to sit the Law National Admissions Test (LNAT). These are University of Bristol; University of Cambridge; Durham University; University of Glasgow; King's College, London (KCL); London School of Economics and Political Science (LSE); University of Oxford; University College London (UCL); SOAS University of London. A good strategy, if aiming for any of these nine institutions, would be to ensure that not all five UCAS choices are LNAT universities, so as to reduce risk depending on your LNAT score. If specifically applying to Oxbridge or Imperial College London, these universities are well known for admissions tests.

Potential admissions tests are part of the picture when creating a university list. Other considerations will be the entry requirements – such as the required pre-university grades (e.g. ABB at A level or 32/45 IB points) and whether there are any essential pre-university subjects that are required. To give you a real-life example of this, while typing 'Zoology' into the UCAS website, I can see that the University of Glasgow (Zoology BSc), at the time of writing, require AAB–BBB at A level and at least one of the subjects needs to be biology or chemistry. Something to note about the grade ranges (e.g. AAB–BBB as seen above): the range is often there to show what's available for contextual offers. Over the last few years, some universities have reduced their requirements for applicants who they feel are somewhat disadvantaged (e.g. from low income backgrounds). So, also note this and check whether it applies. To be safe, my advice is to consider the highest grade as what you need to be focused on. If students are not taking typical pre-university qualifications that are popular in the UK (e.g. A level, International Baccalaureate or Scottish Highers), universities often have specific pages designed for studies expected in other countries. Often it'll be under 'international qualifications' within the entry requirements part of the university's website. Ensure that the predicted grades at least match what the entry requirements are. If you have lower predicted grades then it would not be a strategic choice to apply to the university, as often their first part of the culling process is to send unsuccessful decisions to students who do not meet the basic requirements. The more holistic part of the application decision process, such as reading the personal statement, usually comes slightly later. To be even more strategic in research, students could also check admission success rates (where possible to find) to ensure that they have a balanced range of UCAS choices – some more risky and others a little bit safer.

Offer rates and choosing courses strategically

A new feature that has recently become available on the UCAS website (www.ucas.com) is the option to check the rate of offers for UK school leavers, the most common grades held by accepted students, as well as the range of scores. This can be found at the bottom of the specific course page on UCAS. To again use the example of Zoology, at the University of Glasgow, at the time of writing, AAB at A level was the most common set of grades accepted and the acceptance rate for UK school leavers was 17 in 20. This data can be useful. However, I have also found that on occasion multiple courses that are similar have been mixed in together to make the final dataset and so there should be some caution. In addition, the potential existence of contextual admissions also blurs this data. Nonetheless, do look at this and perhaps not use it as part of the final decision process but do take it into some consideration to give a surface level indication.

TABLE 7 University research table for students – 'reach', 'safe' and 'match' choices.

	Meaning	University	Course name	Grade entry requirements, English requirements and any essential subjects (if applicable)	Is an admissions test required? If so, which one?
Reach	A reach choice is very aspirational – at the top end of your choices – due to it being very competitive in terms of no. of applicants vs. no. of places, in addition to high grade requirements.				
Match	A match choice is where you comfortably meet the entry requirements (maybe even have predicted grades that are slightly higher than required). There is also slightly less competition in terms of application success rates.				
Safe	A safe choice will be a course that is lower than your predicted grades and not a G5 university. It could, in some cases, be a Russell Group, but still ideally less competitive overall compared to your match choice.				

The strategy of having what are known as 'reach', 'safe' and 'match' choices is widely used. Applicants should look at their predicted grades and balance this against the entry requirements and application success rates. If you are a student reading this book, I have included a table that you can write in to note down some early examples of suitable university courses for you. See Table 7.

3 Developing your super-curricular profile

What's available?

Super-curricular profile-building – taking part in relevant academic activities outside of the classroom – is second to none in terms of what's most important in separating yourself from the competition when creating an attention-grabbing personal statement that gets you noticed. Universities, especially highly competitive ones, often advise that students secure such activities as they actively look for evidence of super-curricular experiences when assessing candidates. Whether a student is aiming for a G5, Russell Group, highly competitive or what might be deemed a slightly less competitive university, this should not impact the quality of the personal statement or overall UCAS application. In other words, I think all students, wherever they're aiming, should treat their personal statements with an equal level of enthusiasm in wanting this to be the very best reflection of their academic passion and developed skillset. As mentioned previously in this book, the University of Cambridge recommends that roughly 80% of the UCAS personal statement involves super-curricular content. Recently, University College London told me 75%–85%. A university will not necessarily count the number of words used and calculate a 'super-curricular percentage'; these are just a rule of thumb. Aim for roughly three-quarters. My advice would be to follow the most rigorous examples of what a university is looking for (whether or not you are actually making an application to that specific institution) and this will ensure that your personal statement will be of the highest standard and thus well-suited to impress any university you ultimately choose.

Defining super-curricular

When identifying relevant super-curricular activities, it is crucial to first confidently know what is meant by the term 'super-curricular'. Anything that a student does outside of their classroom subjects, I would call 'co-curricular'. Underneath the umbrella term of 'co-curricular', there are two branches. The first branch is 'extra-curricular' and the second is 'super-curricular'. Non-academic activities, such as sports and music, are known as 'extra-curricular' and academic activities, such as relevant wider reading and attending guest lectures, are known as 'super-curricular'. The additional caveat to super-curricular is that the activity should not only be academic in nature, but also specifically link to the student's university course aspirations. So, if a student wanted to study music and was having piano lessons, this would, in fact, be super-curricular rather than extra-curricular. To give another example, if a student wanted to apply to study Architecture, then a good super-curricular activity might include visiting London's Design Museum to learn more about architectural design. An extra-curricular example for this hypothetical Architecture applicant might include being part of the school's rugby team. Figure 5 (overleaf) offers a breakdown of these terms with some general examples.

Building a super-curricular profile

Now that we are fully aware of what is meant by super-curricular activities, the search can begin to see what is available and then to start participating in such activities to develop a list of experiences (thus, engaging in 'super-curricular profile-building'). From my experience, especially with very conscientious students, they will always have more super curricular experiences than they can actually use in their personal statement. On average, I think a good number of super-curricular activities to secure would be around 10–15. Students may not include all of these experiences, but it offers a tasty platter from which the best fitting super-curricular activities for the personal statement can be lifted. Note that variety is not just the spice of life but also essential seasoning for a winning UCAS personal statement. Therefore, out of the 15 or so super-curricular activities, this should not be made up of 10 books and five podcasts. That's not much variety. To help the personal statement best showcase academic

FIGURE 5: A breakdown of co-curricular experiences (extra-curricular and super-curricular).

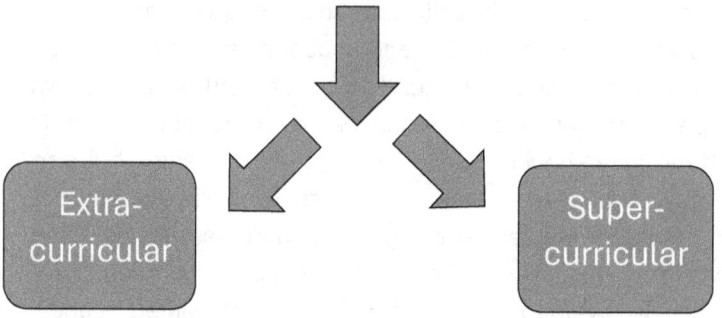

Anything that a student does outside of the classroom, aside from their academic subjects, are known as co-curricular activities.

Extra-curricular is non-academic and/or not linked to the university course the student is applying to. Typical examples may include sports, music, non-academic hobbies and interests.

While not as important as super-curricular, in terms of personal statement overall content, they are still of course worthwhile activities and help showcase roundedness – participating in wider life outside of academia. Useful in particular for Question 3 of the personal statement.

Super-curricular is academic and must also be linked to the university course the student is applying to. There are lots of examples for how one can engage with their future course outside of the classroom – e.g. wider reading; guest lectures; essay and other academic competitions; podcasts; relevant museum visits; relevant work experience; participating in independent projects.

The majority of the personal statement should revolve around super-curricular content.

passion and curiosity (as well as to be an interesting read for the admissions tutor), there needs to be a broad range of different super-curricular activities. Moreover, there is a balance to strike in terms of the overall number of super-curricular activities that should be included in the personal statement. Choosing too many, due to the limit of a 4,000-character personal statement total, might make the writing too descriptive and thus it'll become more of a list of activities rather than an engaging piece of writing. Adding not enough super-curricular activities may raise some red flags as it can indicate a lack of motivation or time management.

Balancing all of these, as another rule of thumb to add into the mix, I would recommend that a personal statement should have around eight different super-curricular activities included. It is OK if one or two are the same type of super-curricular (e.g. two books) but generally there should be eight different types. (As you would agree, the exact super-curricular number will vary based on writing style, specific experiences and the university course – take eight as a rough benchmark with some wiggle room.)

The answer to the question of what's available for super-curricular opportunities is very much down to the individual student – for example, willingness to travel or financial support should there be paid experiences such as summer schools. However, what I am very pleased to inform you is that no matter the budget or university course focus, every student can easily secure that golden number of 10–15 super-curricular activities which will then be whittled down to eight for the final personal statement. Even without any financial backing, as most super-curricular activities can be completed free of charge. From this list of 10–15 activities, students will then be able to pick and choose as to what's most appropriate for the personal statement. Some super-curricular activities are openly advertised and thus easy to take part in. For instance, there are plenty of free online courses related to different subject areas. One of the best online course providers, what are also known as massive open online courses (MOOCs), is www.edx.org. Here, you type in the university course (e.g. 'Mathematics' or 'Philosophy') and then you are presented with mostly a large number of online courses to choose from. These courses, on the edX website, are created by internationally renowned universities. The edX platform often charges for certificates or for extras, such as to keep the class materials, but otherwise, from what I have seen, it is entirely free to complete the online course. This is just one example of many – it often does not take too long or much innovation to secure very interesting and relevant super-curricular opportunities.

Putting the emphasis on students rather than schools to source experiences

Naturally, while school careers advisers, university counsellors and the like will point students in the right direction for relevant super-curricular activities, the emphasis should be placed on the student to remain up-to-date as to what's available. Ways to stay updated may include being on subject-specific mailing lists and checking news and opportunities from bodies representing the field. Bodies may include, as an example, the Royal Institute of British Architects (RIBA) or the British Psychological Society (BPS). It of course depends on the field. In addition, the power of networking can never be understated and so it would be useful to attend open guest lectures, conferences and other events to ask for super-curricular recommendations. Some networking could also take place online (e.g. with a LinkedIn account). I am constantly impressed with what has been secured from building relationships and at least simply done by asking nicely. Examples of really amazing opportunities, sourced through the power of networking, may include participating in relevant research; work experience (more of this in the next section); access to early peer-reviewed articles. A particular highlight that comes to mind is the example of a student last year, at Cardiff Sixth Form College Cambridge, who built, with the help of internal and external academic staff, what is believed to be the first nuclear reactor produced in a school environment. (The achievements of the student, Cesare Mencarini, have since been widely published in the media, such as by the American Nuclear Society, if you wanted to read more about this). As you can see, the opportunities are endless! Finally, use universities to your advantage. Whether you apply to a specific university, many institutions have very useful recommended reading lists and other super-curricular suggestions divided by course choice. Naturally, you do not have to apply to the university to use their resources.

Ways in which schools can foster a super-curricular environment and create opportunities

While the overall onus remains on school students to research super-curricular activities and to remain abreast of subject-specific research and news and so on, school staff and families do also play a role. Whether this be keeping students motivated or pointing them in the right direction of available opportunities. Furthermore, school staff are able to play an even more active role in creating super-curricular experiences. In one of my previous schools where I worked, Oxford International College, they actually have an entire department dedicated to this (aptly named the Supercurricular Department). But even without the opulence of a dedicated team, schools can create their own opportunities nonetheless. Examples may include helping students to establish subject-specific societies (e.g. 'MedSoc' or 'Archaeology Appreciation Society'). Schools may be involved with academic competitions (e.g. a Mathematics Olympiad or various essay competitions). Helping to run trips, such as to Sigmund Freud's house in London, or the MINI Plant in Oxford, are another way to give students opportunities which are very much outside of the classroom but supported by the school.

Again, emphasising the point of using universities to your advantage, schools should be reaching out to universities to help create and maintain strong relationships. For example, earlier this week, I ran a full-day medical programme for our students that was delivered by a well-known and innovative institution, called St George's University Grenada. The university has a campus in the UK (Newcastle) as well as in the Caribbean. What was fantastic, after asking the university if they would be happy to meet prospective medics and be part of Cardiff Sixth Form College Cambridge's half-term enrichment offering (what we call Enrichment Week), is that the university keenly worked with me to produce a varied programme of workshops and lectures. This was provided to the College entirely free of charge and I have innovated very similar offerings from a broad range of universities over the years. For the school to run an enriching super-curricular programme and for universities to have exposure to a captivated group of interested students is a great symbiotic relationship for all parties involved. Everyone wins. Schools need to support super-curricular profile-building and universities need strong and direct marketing.

Summary

Anything academic and outside of the classroom, thus not directly part of the pre-university qualification the student is taking (e.g. A levels, Scottish Highers or the International Baccalaureate), is a super-curricular activity. These can be found in many places – either from the effort of the school or research from the student.

Whether you are a student reading this or a school staff member, or family of a future university applicant, consider sharing resources and asking each other for suggestions. Figure 6 has a comprehensive checklist for the majority of types of super-curricular activities one could do. Especially useful as a resource for students, tick your way through these to ensure variety in your super-curricular profile.

Super-curricular activities do not only highlight academic passion and time management but also serve as a way to engage and interest the reader. Therefore, in line with this by-product of being interesting, it is important to avoid cliché or repetitive super-curricular examples. For instance, while introductory books such as Guru Madhavan's *Think Like an Engineer* (2015)

FIGURE 6: Super-curricular tick list. In alphabetical order.

- [ ] Academic competitions
- [ ] Clubs and societies
- [ ] Debating relevant topics
- [ ] Fieldtrips and other relevant travel
- [ ] Guest lectures, webinars and conferences
- [ ] Independent projects and research
- [ ] Membership with academic bodies and institutions
- [ ] Museums, galleries and relevant exhibitions
- [ ] Online courses (MOOCs)
- [ ] Podcasts, documentaries and film
- [ ] Submitting an essay (for an external award)
- [ ] Summer schools and half-term programmes
- [ ] University subject masterclasses – see university websites
- [ ] Wider reading
- [ ] Work experience (virtual or in-person)

or Henry Marsh's 2014 memoir as a brain surgeon, called *Do No Harm*, are worth reading for learning purposes, they are heavily overused from the perspective of an admissions tutor reading a large number of personal statements. Therefore, consider being creative – either by sourcing rarer examples and/or by offering unique insights when writing about your super-curricular content. One technique to find rarer examples is to identify a niche area of academic interest, such as biomimicry for Architecture or the Late Upper Palaeolithic period for Archaeology, in order to then identify specific academic literature or other super-curricular experiences that go deeper and will be less used than overarching introductory material. Naturally, there is a time and a place for more common super-curricular activities, too; just consider how you use these in the context of wanting to separate yourself from the competition.

Work experience is achievable for all

The importance of work experience (sometimes called a 'work placement' or 'work observation') varies across university courses. For instance, work experience is often an essential requirement for Veterinary Science. Universities for Veterinary Science will request a minimum number of weeks of work experience and some will even go further to specify the types of experiences (e.g. animal handling vs. customer facing). There are currently 11 vet schools in the UK and so check the requirements and cross-reference against what works best for you should you be choosing Veterinary Science.

Other university courses, such as Medicine, may have a strong preference for work experience to be part of the super-curricular profile but do not have this as an essential prerequisite of being made an offer to study at their university. In actual fact, there are many courses (ranging from History to Computer Science) where work experience may be seen as slightly less relevant. As an educator and careers professional for students, my personal approach is that work experience should be completed by all students. This is not only for personal statement material, but also because having a tangible experience of the workplace is useful to develop an understanding of the world of work and thus has benefits from this perspective of self-development. It can also be beneficial to experience particular career sectors and explore how these match your personal preferences and skill sets to help make a best-fit university course decision for the future (especially if you are going down a vocational university course route). Putting all of this to one side and going back to the UCAS personal statement, I still buy into the notion of 'work experience for all', as no matter your course choice, participating in work experience amplifies transferable skills – for example, time management and people skills (sometimes called 'soft skills'). While writing this paragraph, I have been tempted to include a new table to rate the importance of work experience for different university courses. On balance, I have decided against this as while there is an overall difference in the importance of work experience, it also depends on which other super-curricular activities the student has in their profile and which work experience opportunities become available. For instance, a History applicant on the whole might be less likely to include work experience in their personal statement. Nevertheless, should an opportunity arise to spend a week in a museum helping with a relevant exhibition, this would be a fantastic experience to write about. So, in short, I would say that everyone should aim for work experience but balance this against how long it would take you to secure such an opportunity and the need of this for your chosen course. Work experience should be related to what the student wants to study at university (therefore making it super-curricular), and this is different from volunteering or part-time work (which mostly would be more extra-curricular).

Getting yourself out there is key

When I say that 'work experience is achievable for all', putting this as the subheading for the current section, what I mean is that whether you have the means to buy an experience (there are some work experience providers) or a personal network useful to you (e.g. a parent of a Business and Finance applicant owning their own business and therefore offering a direct opportunity for work experience in the company), all students are in a position to be able to secure some form of work experience. The key is about getting yourself out there, networking where possible and securing opportunities.

There are two types of work experience

I believe that there are two different types of work experience. The first is what I call 'applied' and the other is what I call 'speculative'. Applied work experience refers to advertised opportunities that have an application process, and so the student is applying. An example of this would be HSBC's UK Work Experience Programme. This is an in-person, week-long programme in the summer (for UK Year 10–13 students), with the application this year being between February and March. Applications for this typically involve an online assessment and video interview. Here, this work experience is something established and therefore advertised by the company, with set dates and an application process. There are plenty examples of applied work experience opportunities, offered from a range of organisations. The other type of work experience, known as 'speculative', is vastly different. Here, there are no advertised placements that have set dates with an established programme outline that requires an application. Instead, this relies heavier on networking skills as students directly engage with companies and create their own opportunities. Table 8 shows the differences between applied and speculative work experience opportunities.

TABLE 8: Applied and speculative work experience.

Type of work experience	Overview	How this could be secured
Applied	This is where there are advertised opportunities, often found on company websites, that are offering specific work experience. These work experience placements will often have an established programme outline with set dates and an application process.	Search online to identify advertised work experience opportunities and then complete the application process. This may require a reference and often school staff are happy to support by producing a reference. In addition to searching online, speak with those in the industry to see whether they know of any applied work experience opportunities.
Speculative	This is where there are no work experience placements advertised as such. Instead, students are identifying what they would like to and where they would like to have some work experience and they are directly reaching out to relevant companies to try and secure a placement.	Speculative applications require a proactive networking approach. Identify the geographical area and search which relevant companies are there. After which, reach out to these companies by phone and email. Ideally, phoning first (or even visiting in person). Send a CV and cover letter email and follow up to see whether an experience would be possible.

I would recommend following a series of steps to source a speculative work experience. This is outlined in Figure 7. In short, this process involves identifying what is available and then methodically contacting relevant companies in the hope of finding a mutually beneficial time and series of responsibilities so that this works for both parties. Often students will feel apprehensive about approaching companies. In part, I believe this is because students are under the impression that visiting the company and being there for a week or so is rather burdensome and is ultimately a favour that the company is doing for them. I would recommend to think about this differently. For instance, how can the student add value to the company? Well, if a staff member is responsible for the student, this may help the staff member as it shows responsibility and possibly other skills which could contribute to the negotiation of securing a promotion. Some work experiences may simply involve shadowing and so just observing but others may have a hands-on element. Even if considered menial, such as paper shredding or filling, this adds value to the company by assisting with their tasks and overall positive workflow. It does help complete what's needed. Some companies may use the example of offering work experience to show corporate responsibility and outreach, enhancing their marketing. As we can see, there are lots of two-way benefits. Even if the company doesn't have any immediate benefits, they most likely relish the idea of helping the next generation of students who in the future may be part of their industry.

All about CVs

As you can see in Figure 7, contacting companies for speculative work experience requires a CV (sometimes called a résumé) and a cover letter. Starting with the CV (curriculum vitae), this is a short document that gives a summary of your qualifications and experiences. If you search for CV templates, such as in Microsoft Word or Canva, you will get a sense of the overall recommended structure. There is often a logical structure to a CV, which will include a brief introduction, an education section and an experiences section. These are the main components. For an introduction, this will include your name and contact

FIGURE 7: The process of securing speculative work experience.

1. Identify the geographical area where you will begin your search
2. Identify which relevant companies are in the area and build a list of these (including phone numbers)
3. Work your way through the list and phone each company (or even visit in person if possible)
4. When on the phone, briefly introduce yourself and ask whether it would be possible to secure work experience/who would be the right person to speak to about work experience
5. If given an email of someone to contact about work experience, send them an email with a CV and cover letter text (include the details of the person who recommended contacting them)
6. Most likely, by email, if you receive a reply, continue communicating to find the mutually preferred dates to have this work experience (possibly also discussing an overview of the roles and responsibilities)
7. Ensure that your parents/guardians/school are kept informed and they will most likely have to provide consent
8. Repeat this process, in parallel, with a number of companies, to increase the chances of securing a work

details (e.g. phone, email and location), as well as the option of having a short written summary about yourself. Note that, as students may send their CVs to many places, avoid having too many personal details (e.g. date of birth or home address) purely for general good practice and personal data safety. The next section, on education, will include the names of your school(s) and qualifications. Generally, the school does not need to go as far back as primary education and should start from high school/ GCSE or equivalent exams. Name the school, provide the address and outline the qualifications or subjects studied. Note that this should be in reverse chronological order (most recent at the top). Moving on to the experiences section, this should also be in reverse chronological order and detail several notable experiences (e.g. work experience, volunteering, competitions and sports). Have a title for the experience, include the dates and offer a brief description in a sentence or two (or several bullet points). To further amplify your achievements in the experiences section, it is good practice to quantify these. For example, if one experience was that you were the editor of the school magazine, you could include how many articles were published in one of the bullet points. In addition, the experiences section could remain as 'Experiences' as the heading, or, if you have a few examples of specific experiences you could further categorise these into specific headings (e.g. 'Work Experience', 'Academic Competitions', 'Sports'). As you are marketing yourself, tailor the CV to your own experiences. Most students will use the umbrella term of 'Experiences'. Keep your CV to one page. When you progress in your career, during and after university, CV lengths may grow to two or even three pages. It is general convention, however, to keep these short. One page for sixth-form students. See Figure 8 for an example of a CV template. CVs, in terms of style, could be categorised into 'traditional' and 'modern'. Traditional CVs use less colour and infographics, whereas modern CVs make more use of overall graphic design elements. My example, in Figure 8, is mostly traditional but incorporates a combination of a modern format by including a profile picture. You could also think about some infographics to represent skills (e.g. languages and musical instruments) that could be placed under the experiences section. A profile picture is optional. If you do use one, ensure that it is professional – ideally without a distracting background and a headshot facing the camera rather than a full body shot!

Using a cover letter as a customisable email template

From my experience, while this can vary, on average, it can take students around 30 emails to different companies before successfully securing a work experience. Naturally, this number can go up or down depending on the industry and also student approach (plus a bit of luck!). To help emails become scalable and to reach a large audience with minimal effort, a cover letter should have a premade overall structure with some customisability to mention the company name, for example. While in the past a cover letter was attached with a CV and sent in the post, nowadays, with emails, a cover letter takes the form of a customisable email template which is used to, in this case, ask for work experience. I would recommend to have five very short paragraphs/sections

FIGURE 8: CV template example.

Full name at the top

| Optional professional headshot photograph | Contact details here – email; mobile number and city that you're located in |

Introduction

Write some introductory text about yourself – e.g. subject interests for university and that you hope to secure work experience in a relevant field (and why)

Education

- Name of school (dates there for)
  - List the subject/qualifications and if possible include grades in brackets
- Name of school (dates there for)
  - List the subject/qualifications and if possible include grades in brackets

Notable experiences

- Name of the experience (e.g. 'Editor of the school magazine') and provide dates in brackets
  - Have some bullet points to detail the experience
- Repeat
  - Repeat
- Repeat
  - Repeat
- Repeat
  - Repeat

References are available upon request.

FIGURE 9: Cover letter structure.

1. Short introduction to yourself – what do you hope to gain and why.
2. Demonstrate your interest and passion for the subject/industry – e.g. wider reading, attending guest lectures, programmes, society and professional body memberships.
3. What have you done previously and how would this new opportunity build on those experiences?
4. Close by highlighting the importance and interest you place in this opportunity (including a brief reflection about the specific company).
5. Provide dates of your availability. Leave a final comment where you say you would also be available outside of those dates (amplifies your flexibility and desire to be involved).

giving a bit of information about yourself, why you are asking for work experience and when you are available. See Figure 9 for my suggested cover letter structure.

If possible, don't send to generic email addresses

Going back to what I wrote about the number of emails required going up or down based on, in part, the student approach, there are ways to help the email be better placed and thus more likely to receive a positive reply. I would recommend to not use generic email addresses, such as those which do not have a staff member's name (e.g. 'contact@ . . .'; 'enquiries@ . . .'), but instead first phone the company. When answering, you may or may not speak with someone who is in a position to grant the work experience. However, you could do two things: (1) ask whether it's possible to speak with someone directly about work experience; (2) if no one specific is available, ask for the best email to use to contact the individual. Here, hopefully, you'll instead have an email to a specific staff member rather than placing a message into a generic inbox. Students can even start the email by mentioning that they phoned reception and were given this email – which further builds trust and shows motivation early.

Being empowered to create your own opportunities

At Cardiff Sixth Form College Cambridge, while we do have industry contacts, I prefer that students first go through the process of contacting employers themselves. Whether they

3 Developing Your Super-Curricular Profile

are initially successful, to be proactive and develop those communicative and 'go-getter' qualities are impressive skills for life that will be useful. If you are a student, give this a go and fully embrace the chance of creating your own opportunities! As a staff member at a school, consider empowering students – maybe through some CV and cover letter workshops and practice company phone calls – which will pay you back in dividends! With the help of my colleagues, Natalie Ashworth and David Gasper, we run such workshops and provide 1:1 and group feedback. We request that students keep a spreadsheet of their progress in contacting companies. See Table 9 for an example of how this spreadsheet for students could look.

When considering the difference between applied and speculative work experience, both are excellent opportunities and I would recommend attempting both (if available) to further increase the chances of securing work experience. A common question I receive about work experience is which types are available and how long they can last. See Table 10 for an outline

TABLE 9: Work experience companies contact spreadsheet. An adaptable template to help record networking and company interactions.

Name of company and website	Phone number	Main work experience contact and email address	CV and cover letter email sent (tick)	Date of CV and cover letter email	Follow up required? (include date)	Any other notes
			☐			
			☐			
			☐			
			☐			
			☐			
			☐			

TABLE 10: The various types of work experience.

Work experience type	Typical length of time
Workplace visits	One day
Job shadowing	Several days
Insight programmes and Spring Weeks	Between one day and a week
Traditional work placement	One or two weeks
Internship	Several months

of types of work experience and some guidance on the length. Whether one day during the week or one month during the summer, any opportunity to be in the workplace will be extremely valuable and help the personal statement shine. It is not only about what students do and ensuring that there are sufficient super-curricular activities included in the personal statement, but what's also important is how the students write about these activities in a reflective and interesting way. More on recording and writing about super-curricular activities in the next section.

Recording and writing reflectively about your super-curricular activities

Under the previous subheadings, we looked at which super-curricular activities are available and how to secure such opportunities. If you are a school staff member reading this, I would recommend that you meet with each student and possibly use a questionnaire (e.g. Google Forms) to ascertain, as early as possible, which courses students are aiming for and which super-curricular activities they have already taken part in. While the onus is always on students, knowing which super-curricular activities are available/have already been secured should be an open dialogue between all parties (school and student) and embedded in a strong careers programme. Some schools may use data management systems and online services, such as Unifrog, to record super-curricular activities and have shared visibility. My personal approach is to keep a spreadsheet so that no students slip through the net and then ensure that they continue to pursue a range of activities but do not necessarily force this or provide a specific number of activities that they have to complete by a certain date. Then, around four or five months before the personal statement is due, I will review a list of experiences from each student and consider recommending additional super-curricular activities. As a school leader, for better or worse, I am of the firm and on occasion unique belief that 'analysis leads to paralysis' and so, for inspections and overall good practice, it is important to have some documentation but also the flexibility to allow students to feel motivated and less strained to have to tick boxes. Give them the autonomy to participate in super-curricular activities outside the classroom at their own time and their own pace. I think this environment nurtures better outcomes.

Tick lists and reflective journals

One recommendation to ensure that a range of super-curricular activities have been secured is to use the tick list found back in Figure 6. In addition to this, as it is all too easy to forget about some of the past super-curricular experiences or at least to not be able to later reflect as well after the memory is no longer fresh, it could be useful to keep a reflective journal. The reflective journal should be a document that allows students to note which super-curricular activities they've completed – a description of the activity; dates of completion; what was learned and enjoyed; inspiration for following activities. See an example of a reflective journal in Table 11 (overleaf). Note that super-curricular activities need not be conducted only just before the university application – experiences from several years ago, for instance, may still be valid and so these can be included in the reflective journal.

What I mean by inspiration for following activities, is that often super-curricular activities do not happen in isolation. For example, let's say that one of the practical topics within a summer school programme offered a student greater insight into stem cell research. Following this, the student decided to attend a related guest lecture and read the speaker's latest book. This then inspired the student to submit an evaluation of the strengths and limitations of stem cell research for an essay competition. While not all super-curricular activities will be connected in this way, when recording which activities have been completed, it is useful to consider how this activity could inspire another. A great way to show universities that you have subject passion, curiosity and academic prowess is to highlight how one activity inspired another. This also helps with the written flow of the personal statement, in so far as there is less of a 'listing effect' of simply outlining experiences. To show how one activity leads to another, as a personal statement writer, forces you to dissect further how these are connected and why you wanted to learn more.

TABLE 11: A reflective journal for super-curricular activities.

Name of the super-curricular activity (and date completed)	A description of the activity	What did you learn and enjoy from this experience?	How does this link to your future university course? (e.g. skills, knowledge)	Has this inspired you to engage in any other activities? If so, which others and why?

The importance of deep reflection (don't just describe)

If you are someone who has prepared an Extended Project Qualification (EPQ) submission, or completed essay coursework, often you may hear that one of the best ways to enter the higher grade boundaries is to move from being descriptive to more evaluative. In order words, do not just regurgitate what has already been said or simply outline something only from a surface level, but go deeper and provide your own unique insight. While the personal statement is by no means an academic essay, it is important to not simply describe your super-curricular activities (i.e. stating what you've done) but you need to go deeper. Make it interesting and engaging for the reader, while also using the super-curricular experiences as a platform to amplify your skills and passion. Market yourself. Thus, make it easy for the admissions tutor reading your personal statement to have confidence in knowing that you will excel on your chosen course and will add value to the university.

If I was to summarise, in one word, what would be an umbrella term for all that you can do to go beyond describing, it would be 'reflect'. Naturally, you will have to do some describing to explain the super-curricular activity but keep this to a minimum and reflect by writing about what you've learned and enjoyed. How did this experience compare with your academic studies at school or what you have previously read? How did this super-curricular activity show you what may be expected at university and confirm that this is a course you would like to pursue further? Going beyond describing to offering deeper insight and reflecting is not an easy task and so this will take some practice through writing multiple drafts. As a school student, feel free to ask teachers, friends, family and so on to read some of your practice drafts and ask them to imagine being an admissions tutor – have you gone beyond describing to offering some unique and interesting reflection?

Later in this book, in Chapter 7, we have included six specially made examples of complete UCAS personal statements. Figure 10, gives you a snippet from one of these examples (a hypothetical Geography applicant) to show you an example of how related super-curricular activities are incorporated into a single piece of text. Moreover, there is some decent reflection here while not overpowering and crossing the line into becoming an academic essay.

FIGURE 10: A snippet from an exemplar personal statement (highlighting super-curricular variety and adequate reflection).

> 'At the inaugural session of my school's Geography society, I recall a discussion on Dorling's Population 10 Billion. I found his criticism of the carbon trading system convincing, which I later found to be supported by an LSE study that showed Dorling's push for a progressive tax system could minimise environmental costs without restricting growth. His method, I argue, provides an effective way to rein in carbon emissions, and a hybrid model consisting of a cap on emissions and a price ceiling for carbon permits may be the best remedy.'

It is not to say that all personal statements have to be written in the exact style as seen in Figure 10 (after all, each personal statement needs to be relatively unique and reflect the applicant's own voice), but this does showcase a tangible example which may offer a useful comparison to your own drafts. In the example, you can see that the applicant starts by dropping in the first super-curricular, not by saying that he's a member of the Geography Society, but by starting the sentence by outlining a relevant discussion. This is subtle and strategic – it is more interesting to implicitly imply what you have gained from an experience than outrightly introducing the fact that you are a member of a society and then going into the reflection (e.g. 'Since last year, I have been a member of my school's Geography Society. During my time, I have come across . . .'). The applicant reflected by stating that he was intrigued by the criticism and then compared this to another super-curricular (wider reading in the form of an LSE study). The applicant did not stop there but went in with some further insight by describing the results of the study (showing good subject knowledge) and then providing an evaluative point (the reflection). Note that a reflection does not always need to be evaluative in nature, but it is one option. Figure 11 gives some examples of how students can be reflective and includes some possible sentence starters for inspiration.

FIGURE 11: Possible sentence starters for reflections in the personal statement.

- 'As I reflect on my involvement in [activity], I've begun to understand the importance of self-directed learning and how it has pushed me to take ownership of my academic interests in [subject].'
- 'Engaging with [activity] has prompted me to reconsider my understanding of [subject], as it allowed me to see how [specific concept or skill] applies beyond the classroom. For example, ...'
- 'In reflecting on my experience with [activity], I've come to understand the value of persistence and adaptability in learning, especially when faced with new or challenging concepts in [subject].'
- 'Looking back on my experiences with [activity], I can see how it has helped me develop a more nuanced understanding of [subject], especially in areas I initially overlooked. For example,...'
- 'My participation in [activity] has made me aware of the gaps in my knowledge and encouraged me to explore areas of [subject] I hadn't considered before. Prompted by what I have learned, it has made me ask questions, such as...'
- 'My passion for [subject] has been further enriched through my involvement in [activity], where I was able to [specific achievement or learning experience].'
- 'One of the key ways I have developed my interest in [subject] is by engaging with [activity], which has broadened my perspective on [related topic], by...'
- 'Participating in [activity] has led me to question some of the ideas I had about [subject] and pushed me to challenge my own thinking in new ways. For example,...'
- 'The more I explored [activity], the more I realised that my fascination with [subject] extends beyond just theoretical knowledge; I now feel motivated to apply what I've learned in real-world situations.'
- 'There are several key skills that I have developed for university study, such as...'
- 'This [topic] contrasted with what I have previously learned as...'
- 'This experience of [activity] has further highlighted that this university course is suited to my passion and interests because...'
- 'Through [activity], I have not only expanded my knowledge of [subject], but also enhanced my critical thinking by [mention specific learning or skill gained].'
- 'Through my engagement with [activity], I've realised how much I enjoy the challenge of tackling complex problems, which has made me rethink how I approach learning in [subject].'
- 'Through my involvement in [activity], I've become more aware of the connections between theory and practice, which has given me a new lens through which to view [subject].'
- 'Through my involvement in [activity], I've come to realise how much more there is to learn about [subject], and how this experience has challenged my previous assumptions. For instance,...'
- 'What intrigued me most about [activity], was...'

4   The writing

Tackling question 1: 'Why do you want to study this course or subject?'

Now that we have fully looked at super-curricular profile-building, we should have the content (or at least be in a position to know what the content involves). Content not only comes in the form of super-curricular activities but also some personal anecdotes and information that can convince the reader that the applicant has thought about this well and believes that their chosen university course is the right next step for them. Admitting students and providing conditional offers involves admission tutors making a decision regarding the best fit – naturally, universities would not want to make offers to students who are not motivated or do not possess transferable skills that will increase the chances of successfully completing the university course. After all, universities are not only places of education but are also charities and businesses; they would want to reduce dropout rates and do their best to enhance student satisfaction scores. Moreover, if you have been made an offer from a university for a course that you are not suited to, this is not beneficial for you either and so, from the discussions I have had, universities are keen to offer a fair assessment with students' interests in mind too. Couple this outlook with the realisation of supply and demand (for many competitive university courses, demand outstrips supply), we can all agree that the first question within the personal statement needs to grab the attention of the reader from the outset. Remember that the three questions which make up the UCAS personal statement are not read in isolation and this first question can be seen as the introduction and a part of the main body.

In terms of structure, the personal statement (all three questions) should be written in formal prose with the use of paragraphs. Interestingly, often students will draft the personal statement with usual paragraphs but then, when pasting their draft into the UCAS portal, they remove the spaces between paragraphs. This is because of the character count! Often, it can become that close where removing the spaces cuts the personal statement down to what's required (a maximum of 4,000). Another tip, in relation to this, is to double-check that there are no extra spaces at the end of each paragraph or full stop. It makes a big difference to your total character count when removing these unnecessary spaces!

When starting the writing process, it may feel rather daunting to have to fill 4,000 characters; however, in actual fact, roughly 95% of all the personal statements I have seen, towards the middle stage of drafting, go well beyond the 4,000 maximum. Totals such as 6,000 or so are not uncommon! Anyway, in my opinion, it is far easier to cut down when you've written much of what you would like to include rather than not having enough material to fill the space and then struggling to add more content. While it is not inconceivable to start working on one question of the personal statement and then dipping in and out in the drafting process, as a general rule, I would suggest starting with Question 1 first and then moving on to Question 2 and finally ending with the drafting of Question 3. Starting with Question 1 allows you to set the scene and identify the 'thread'/themes that you would like to maintain throughout the entire personal statement. However, of course, everyone is different and so ultimately students should follow their gut – whether they'd like to start with Question 1 or otherwise.

As I suggest starting with Question 1 first, this subheading within this section of the book, even though it looks at Question 1, will also contain some information about all three questions, as you need to be aware of this as you progress throughout the personal statement writing. Especially at the time of writing, when applicants are only getting used to the new personal statement structure for the 2026 cycle, it can be confusing to be sure as to which content goes where in terms of the three questions. Moreover, it can also be unclear as to how you should divide the character count between questions. What is certain is that universities, as well as guidance from UCAS more generally, give applicants free rein as to the decision of how many characters per section (although there is a 350-character minimum requirement for each question). In addition, universities so far have informed me that they are happy to see super-curricular and other valuable content interspersed in whichever question. So, in many ways, at least on the surface, this is a blank canvas. However, speaking even closer with universities and also incorporating some of my own experience, I think the new personal statement questions in many ways replicate the original free-text structure (an example can be found on **pages 10–11**). The first question very much lends itself to the usual introduction of amplifying the crystallising moment of why you have selected the course followed by some main body super-curricular evidence. The third question is more along the lines of non-academic activities to showcase other parts of your personality and skill set (extra-curricular). It has always been suggested that extra-curricular activities, while useful, should be significantly less of the overall character count than the meatier academic passion and curiosity. Therefore, while there is some flexibility, you are most likely reading this book wanting some vivid and carefully considered advice, information and guidance. Out of the 4,000 total character count, I would recommend to have around 50%–60% characters for Question 1; 30%–40% Question 2; 10% Question 3. See Table 12 for an outline of how many characters and the overall suggested content for each personal statement question. See also Figure 12 (overleaf) for my top eight overall pieces of advice how to make your personal statement stand out.

When writing the first sentence of your Question 1, you should be thinking of this as the very first impression. Not only do you want to come across as an applicant who has spent a lot of time, energy and ultimately intelligence on this personal statement, but you want to grab the attention of the reader. The most convincing way that I can think of doing this is to be entirely authentic. Students can do this by providing a unique insight into their genuine academic passion and curiosity. In other words, shed some light on the 'crystallising' moment where you realised that rather than any other university course, you have chosen to spend the next three years or more of your life dedicated to this academic field. For some examples of crystallising moments, you can look at the six personal statement examples found towards the end of this book. The economics personal statement in Chapter 7, points to the example of growing up in a gold shop and being captivated by consumer behaviour along with the factors surrounding gold as

TABLE 12: A breakdown of the three personal statement questions.

Question	Suggested character count (% of 4,000 total)	Suggested content
1. 'Why do you want to study this course or subject?'	2,000–2,400 (50–60%)	An interesting and engaging opening paragraph, outlining the reasons you would like to study this course. Several main body style paragraphs, including significant super-curricular content written with a reflective approach to highlight academic knowledge, subject passion and curiosity. Consider including personal anecdotes and topic themes to build a convincing narrative.
2. 'How have your qualifications and studies helped you to prepare for this course or subject?'	1,200–1,600 (30–40%)	Mostly looking at your pre-university subjects (e.g. A levels) and how these have peaked your interest and prepared you for university. Consider also including some super-curricular content that link well to this question. Remember not to list your current subjects or spend too many characters describing the subjects. Not all pre-university subjects have to be included here.
3. 'What else have you done to prepare outside of education, and why are these experiences useful?'	400 (10%)	Here you are showing your roundness as a candidate outside of academia – how will you add to the social fabric of the university? What other skills and interests can you bring? This is where most of the extra-curricular content will be housed. However, relevant undertones of academic passion, curiosity and best fit can still come through.

Note: These are general recommendations, and the personal statement, including character count, can still be shaped slightly differently depending on the applicant's style.

a commodity. Figure 13 (overleaf) offers some further examples for inspiration as to what could constitute a crystallising moment – your personal anecdote relating to the reason for what ignited or at least catalysed your decision to go down your chosen path of university study above all other options.

In terms of Question 1 structure, following your opening paragraph, I would then recommend having a paragraph (or several paragraphs) dedicated to super-curricular activities to

FIGURE 12: Eight ways to make your personal statement stand out.

1. Quality rather than quantity – do not simply list and briefly describe experiences but expand on these in a reflective and interesting way
2. Originality (plagiarism is an offence at university) – UCAS have a similarity report check built in and there's nothing to stop universities doing their own analysis
3. Find your 'thread' – embed themes/topics that you use throughout the personal statement to best highlight your academic passion and curiosity
4. Have strong substance (build a portfolio of experiences, perhaps through a reflective journal) – super-curricular content is key
5. Not just breadth but also depth of knowledge – to further distinguish yourself ensure that you show a detailed understanding beyond the introductory level
6. Highlight your strengths – ultimately, you are selling yourself and so avoid overly discussing any weaknesses or limitations you feel you may have
7. Hyperbolic is better than indifference – you shouldcome across in your choice of writing as motivated and therefore excited about the course and university life
8. Captivating writing style – consider how many personal statements admissions tutors read; use tone, structure and quality of writing to make your piece shine

evidence your academic passion and curiosity. When earlier, I mentioned the concept of a 'thread', what I was referring to is a common theme being embedded – such as the example of gold in the Economics personal statement provided in this book. For continuity, driving home a narrative and overall good structure, it would be useful to have one or more threads. The Economics example goes heavy on the use of gold and so look at this as an example but feel free, of course, to deviate from this with a heavy dose of your personal style. The thread does not need to be this strong. Instead of a continuous thread, for example, you may just want to identify some themes that make up the main body – for example an interest in cutting-edge research, applying subject theory to real-world examples such as industry and the world of work; useful practical applications; case studies of previous academic achievements in the field. It is these themes that you can, if you choose to, launch in the introduction and then return to these in the super-curricular main body paragraphs.

FIGURE 13: Examples of possible crystallising moments drawing you to your chosen university course (which can be expanded on in the personal statement).

Passion for the subject: expressing a deep, personal interest in the subject is crucial. Share why you find the topic exciting, engaging or intellectually stimulating. For example, if you're applying to study History, you could mention how specific events or historical periods have always fascinated you and inspired your academic curiosity.

Career aspirations: relating the subject to your long-term career goals shows that you're thinking about the future and how the degree will help you reach your ambitions. For example, if you're applying for Medicine, discuss how a passion for the underpinning science or an experience with healthcare sparked your interest in the field.

Skills and strengths: highlighting how your personal skills align with the subject can make a strong case for your suitability. For example, if you're applying for Engineering, you could talk about how your problem-solving abilities or love for working with technology made you choose the course.

Academic achievements and experiences: mentioning how your academic history has prepared you for the subject can demonstrate your dedication. For instance, if you've excelled in relevant subjects (such as Biology for a Veterinary Science application), explain how these experiences have solidified your decision to pursue the university course.

Personal and super-curricular experiences: relating real-life experiences that have influenced your decision to study the course can make your personal statement stand out. For instance, if you have volunteered or worked in an area related to the subject (e.g. volunteering at a charity for social work), explain how these experiences deepened your interest in the field.

Desire to contribute to society: if you're interested in subjects like social sciences, environmental studies or healthcare, you could explain your desire to contribute to solving global challenges, improving communities or making a difference in people's lives.

Curiosity and lifelong learning: expressing a desire for continual learning and intellectual development can demonstrate your commitment to academic growth. If you're applying to a subject like Philosophy or Mathematics, you could describe how the subject challenges you to think critically and push the boundaries of your knowledge.

Inspiration from role models: if a teacher, mentor or public figure has inspired you to pursue a particular field, you could mention this at the crystallising moment. Explain how their influence motivated you to choose the course and how you aspire to follow a career path or perhaps contribute in a similar way.

Challenges or obstacles overcome: if there's a personal story or challenge that has led you to choose the course, sharing this can add depth and authenticity to your personal statement. For example, overcoming a personal health challenge and deciding to study Medicine or Psychology could resonate strongly with admissions tutors.

Relevance to current issues: linking the subject to current global or societal issues can show that you're aware of the world around you. For example, applying for PPE or International Relations might involve discussing your following of geopolitical events or how you want to contribute to finding solutions.

Whether you are a member of staff at a school reading this or a current student, you will be familiar with recommending paragraph structures to help organise thoughts and ensure that paragraphs are not just descriptive but offer something deeper and more interesting. Examples of these critical paragraph scaffolds include PEE (starting with a Point, then Evidence, then an Explanation) and what is often used in English essays, PETAL (Point, Evidence, Technique, Analysis, Link). When I was recently at the UCAS Annual Conference for Teachers and Advisers, they recommended a personal statement paragraph structure of PEEL (Point, Evidence, Explanation, Link). See Figure 14 for a PEEL example. Whether you choose a specific critical paragraph scaffold, keep in mind the essential ingredients that all of these scaffolds contain and use this insight to construct several of your own main body paragraphs. Remember, if you have a reflective journal, feel free to copy and paste your notes from here and you can edit these notes to fill out a more complete paragraph. Even better still, perhaps you have already used a paragraph structure in your reflective journal of super-curricular activities and so this will make the writing process even more seamless!

FIGURE 14: Breaking down the PEEL structure with a paragraph example.

P = Point → Generate an idea, theme or topic you would like to introduce → e.g. 'My passion for architecture stems from a deep fascination with the way built environments shape human experiences and communities.'

E = Evidence → Reinforce this with super-curricular activitiesor other experiences → e.g. 'I have actively engaged with architectural projects through internships and independent study. During a summer placement at a local architectural firm, I assisted in the design process, helping create 3D models and collaborating on client presentations.'

E = Explanation → Expand on this with somemore information and an interesting reflection → e.g. 'This experience not only enhanced my technical skills, such as using software like AutoCAD and SketchUp, but also highlighted the significance of balancing creativity with practicality. I saw first hand how architects must consider both aesthetic value and the functionality of spaces, ensuring they meet the needs of users while adhering to environmental and structural constraints.'

L = Link → Bring this back to the university course in a way that nods to your passion, suitability or perceived value in such a degree → e.g. 'This understanding motivates me topursue a degree in Architecture, where I can further refine my design abilities and contribute to the creation of sustainable and innovative spaces that have a positive impact on society.'

Question 1 is the place where you engage with an insightful opening paragraph and then provide several main body paragraphs with high-quality super-curricular content. Remember not to list experiences but to reflect on what you have learned from your super-curricular activities and market yourself effectively by using these reflections to highlight relevant skills and attributes relevant to the chosen course. This section should exude academic passion and curiosity. Remember that the tone should be academic but not as far as an evaluative essay – keep it formal with overtones of interesting reflection that would be suitable for subject experts and more general readers alike. Some universities and courses start with general personal statement readers who filter these into a next round where they are then passed to subject-specific academic staff. So, while the reader will take the form of an admissions tutor from the university, ensure that this personal statement is suitable for both subject experts and individuals who are experts with personal statements but may not have the academic background should you be using lots of key terminology and theory without detailing what you mean. Key terminology and subject knowledge relevant to the field are very important to include, however, so find a balance between incorporating this knowledge to the point where it is mostly understandable to both learned but general readers too.

Tackling question 2: 'How have your qualifications and studies helped you to prepare for this course or subject?'

Question 2, while still something I would consider a main body paragraph section that should be seasoned with relevant super-curricular, has in many ways deviated from the previous advice regarding high-quality and competitive personal statements. Generally speaking, the idea of spending a chunk of characters detailing your current qualifications was counterintuitive. Namely, this is because the universities are already aware of the applicant's academic profile as their qualifications (both previously achieved and currently undertaken with the denotation of predicted grades) are outlined within the overall UCAS application. Space, therefore, should be saved for diving into relevant super-curricular activities.

However, it is not uncommon for applicants to touch upon their current studies as a way of showing their preparedness for future university studies. This could be done by making a direct link – for example, referring to A level Economics when applying to study a degree in Economics. This could also be made with a link not in terms of subject to subject but of relevant cross-over – for example, looking at the benefits of History A level in the context of preparedness for a degree in Philosophy (perhaps pointing to essay writing skills or critical thinking ability). Links between your current school qualifications could be based on the actual subject material learned and how this applies but also on the useful skills or new perspectives the lens of the school subject has afforded you in relation to considering the nature of your future university course.

Question 2 offers applicants the chance to look deeper into their school studies and bring this experience into the mix when marketing their suitability for their chosen university course. In the same way, I previously mentioned that it was common guidance not to waste too many characters on outlining the school qualifications (universities can already see your list of qualifications in the application), do not simply describe what you have done in class or learned overall but be creative in applying these qualifications and studies to the university course. On the one hand, Question 2 could start with you identifying specific topics from your school subject, or you could go straight to your subject overall and how these offer transferable skills. For example, again drawn from the full personal statement examples found towards the end of this book, an IB applicant applying for undergraduate Medicine may start with: 'Studying English B HL, I learnt the art of communication, the importance of argument construction and the need for thought clarity.' Identifying relevant topics and then later going into more detail about the link, an A level applicant applying for Geography may start by writing: 'Throughout Geography A level I have enjoyed modules on geopolitics and technological innovation to combat environmental issues . . .'

I do think that Question 1 should absolutely have the most number of characters, as seen in my suggested character division in Table 12. In part, this is due to the bulk of super-curricular activities being housed there. Having said this, super-curricular activities can also be provided in Question 2. As we can see in the personal statement question, 'How have your qualifications and studies helped you to prepare for this course or subject?', this is broadly put. 'Studies', for example, need not just be in the classroom and so this does open up the possibility of studies from outside the classroom (i.e. super-curricular content). Consider bringing in some super-curricular activities that have studying at the core – for example, an online course or essay competition rather than work experience or a school trip. As you can see in the later personal statement examples, there is a way of weaving in relevant super-curricular activities to bolster the overall discussion surrounding qualifications and studies. As we know that the personal statement will be read as a single document with the three questions combined, repeating activities and experiences from Question 1 into Question 2 should in most cases be avoided. On occasion, for useful repetition or to provide a new critical evaluation/reflection, the same content may be drawn upon but of course used in a different way.

Tackling question 3: 'What else have you done to prepare outside of education, and why are these experiences helpful?'

As we progress throughout the personal statement questions, this third and final one, I would suggest, would most likely have the least number of characters compared to Question 2 and most definitely compared to Question 1. Universities want to ensure that students are academically a good fit but also that they will contribute to the social fabric of the institution. To help showcase your roundedness as an applicant, here is the space for some extra-curricular pursuits. Remember that extra-curricular, as opposed to super-curricular, are activities that are not academic or not linked to your university course choice. Examples may include sports, music, other hobbies and interests. Volunteering work could also go here. This is not just the home of extra-curriculars per se and other interesting points can be included here. Nevertheless, I would recommend that this should mostly be used for activities and experiences that are less likely to be included in Question 1 or Question 2.

TABLE 13: How the personal statement examples link extra-curricular in Question 3 to suitability for the course and/or for university life.

Personal statement example	Example of extra-curricular content	How this was linked to suitability for the course and/or for university life
Example 1	Volunteering with Age Concern	An understanding of generational perspectives and current affairs (useful for the course and the variety of views at university)
Example 2	Gymnastics and knitting	Maintaining work-life balance; enhancing manual dexterity (usual for Medicine)
Example 3	Learning Mandarin; an interest in music and sports	Mandarin gives access to material not in English (useful for a more global understanding of Economics); broad sports and music shows holistic ability for being involved in wider university life
Example 4	Attended a talk by a Foreign Correspondent for BBC News	Highlighted potential career aspirations of being in the Media and the role that philosophy plays in presenting and analysing complex arguments
Example 5	Travelling while sketching and taking photographs	An fascination with various buildings observed during travel and highlighting an interest in art though drawing and photography
Example 6	Karate (and being an instructor)	Relating qualities for sports (e.g. resilience, perseverance and dedication) to the study of Computer Science; Communication skills from being an instructor to writing code

What often impresses me is the way students are able to use the extra-curricular activities to then link this back to the university course. A classic example would be a medical applicant, who enjoys drawing or playing the piano and then can use this to amplify their suitability for Medicine, such as in terms of practising manual dexterity. Volunteering is another example, which could be linked to vocational courses that require possibly working with vulnerable individuals (should the specific volunteering experience lend itself in that way). The key is that while you are showing your roundness as a candidate outside of academia, relevant undertones of academic passion, curiosity and best fit can still come through in Question 3. Table 13 provides the specific examples, from the full personal statements found at the back of this book, of how extra-curricular examples have been linked to suitability for the course and/or for university life.

There is no one-size-fits-all approach, as such, as personal statements are all unique. Over the last decade or so, I have seen personal statements that are very conventional in style and lead to extremely successful outcomes in terms of university offers. Equally, on the other side, I have seen extremely unconventional personal statements do well (one, for example, as I mentioned earlier in this book, mostly involved writing about the Iron Man character which received an Oxbridge offer). Of course, the latter strategy is far riskier and you should express extreme caution. The best strategy, would be to follow some convention but of course add your own spin with an engaging writing style and uniquely insightful reflections – after all, putting the personal into personal statement. Some convention, such as a heavy emphasis on super-curricular content and doing well to expand on these in an interesting and well-written style are unshakeable features that must be in there. Question 1 requires interesting an engaging reasons as to why this course is for you (consider using personal anecdotes to hook the reader) and draw upon some themes bolstered by super-curricular main body paragraphs. Question 2 brings in your academic qualifications and studies – what you are currently studying now – linking these to the university course and still being original in identifying how these sell you as a desirable applicant. Super-curricular can still be used in this question. The final question, Question 3, houses extra-curricular content but still returns back to reasons for the course and/or university study and wider university life. Use the six personal statement examples found in Chapter 7 to see how all of this comes together.

5 After writing

Stepping away and then stepping forward

When you have completed a full UCAS personal statement that you are happy with, there is still some unfinished business. Firstly, congratulate yourself on implementing many of your super-curricular activities and unique insights into a cohesive and convincing piece of writing that best reflects your skills, attributes, experiences and personality. I use the words 'finished' or 'completed' lightly, as while the bulk of this completed draft may remain unchanged, take some time to step away before going back to your writing to reread and consider any final changes – whether it's some rephrasing of a few sentences or adding one or two new experiences.

Imagine yourself as an admissions tutor

When students return to their personal statements with fresh eyes, they'll be able to see the reality of what they have written as opposed to what they thought was there at the time of being immersed in the writing process. Moreover, now that they have a complete draft available, they can inspect their personal statement in full. An important part of what I call stepping away and then stepping forward is to take yourself out of the perspective of a writer and into a reader. More specifically, imagine yourself as an admissions tutor for a selective university. Consider what they would believe to be the essential and desirable characteristics of a high-quality personal statement and assess yourself against these criteria. It is not just the personal statement writer who can imagine being an admissions tutor – applicants could also ask friends, family, school staff and maybe even those connected within the academic field to read the personal statement through the lens of a potential admissions tutor. Figure 15 has a checklist that can be used to assess the personal statement against some criteria that admissions tutors may be considering. Ensure that your personal statement has met most, if not all, of these criteria.

5 After Writing

FIGURE 15: A checklist when assessing personal statements (imagining being an admissions tutor). Listed in no particular order.

☐ **1. Academic motivation and passion for the university course**
- **Why you want to study the course:** admission tutors want to see genuine enthusiasm for the subject a rea. They'll look for clear reasons as to why you are interested in it and how you have engaged with it beyond the classroom (i.e. super-curricular activities)
- **Understanding of the course content:** you should demonstrate awareness of what the course entails and show that you've already discovered some areas within the subject area that you find interesting.

☐ **2. Relevant experience and skills**
- **Academic achievements:** your personal statement should highlight relevant subjects, academic achievements or projects that are directly related to the course you're applying for.
- **Transferable skills:** for example, critical thinking, problem-solving, communication, teamwork or leadership are important for many courses. Show how you've developed these skills through various experiences.

☐ **3. Commitment and dedication**
- **Perseverance and motivation:** admissions tutors look for evidence of your commitment to pursuing higher education. This could be shown through overcoming challenges, a consistent work ethic or long-term dedication to your subject or related activities.
- **Self-awareness and reflection:** tutors want to see that you've thought about your academic journey, including any areas of strength or improvement. Reflecting on personal development can demonstrate maturity.

☐ **5. Personal qualities and character**
- **Uniqueness and personality:** tutors want to get a sense of who you are as an individual. A good personal statement should reveal something about your character, your values, academic interests and your approach to challenges.
- **Resilience and adaptability:** show how you've responded to challenges or changes, demonstrating that you can cope with the demands of university life.

☐ **6. Structure and clarity of writing**
- **Well-written and coherent:** the personal statement should be clear, concise and free of errors. Admissions tutors very much appreciate a well-structured statement that is easy to read and follow.
- **Originality and personal voice:** avoid clichés and generic statements. A personal statement that genuinely reflects your experiences, interests and aspirations will stand out more than one that sounds generic or overly rehearsed.

☐ **7. Engagement with the wider world**
- **Awareness of current issues or developments in your field:** this is particularly important for some courses (e.g. Law, Politics, or Medicine). If relevant, mention current trends or issues within your chosen field, showing that you're actively engaging with new ideas and challenges.
- **Cultural awareness and open-mindedness:** being aware of diverse perspectives and demonstrating a broader understanding of the world can be valuable, especially for courses that require critical thinking or collaboration.

☐ **8. Fit with the university and course**
- **Specific interest in the university:** some universities may look for hints that you have researched their courses and facilities. They want to see that you're applying for specific reasons, whether it's, for example, their teaching style, resources or course structure. Remember that you should not name universities directly or alienate others, but you can give subtle hints especially if relevant toall five course choices.
- **Alignment with the academic rigour required:** universities will vary based on academic expectations. Consider your course choices and ensure that you have presented material in the personal statement that shows you can keep up and succeed within such an environment.

Cross-reference the personal statement against the chosen university courses

Students who have completed their personal statements are probably only a month or so away before submitting the UCAS application (which opens from September of each year). Therefore, they should be more convinced in their decision-making process of selecting universities, having done their research – for example, attending open days; university fairs; speaking with friends and family; watching videos made by students about their universities; reading course descriptions and so on. Consequently, students should now be armed with their predicted grades and ideas surrounding what constitutes their best-fit university course. When this university shortlist is more solidified, I would recommend reading and rereading the course page found on the specific university web page. From these course descriptions, consider what skills, attributes, experiences and personality each course may be looking for and cross-reference the personal statement against these. It is not an exact science to be able to ascertain all features that the university would want to see and there are many factors impacting success that are less connected to the personal statement (such as the academic profile of students applying to the course in that particular year), but certainly cross-referencing the style and content of what you've written with an inferred suggestion of what specific universities are looking for can only increase how tailored your personal statement is.

Furthermore, while applicants should not directly name a university that they would like to receive an offer from (e.g. 'I feel that I am suited to the course at X university because . . .'), applicants can strategically mention one or two universities that are on their list of five choices. For example, perhaps there was a relevant webinar, guest lecture or other relevant experience that was held by a specific university. In the context of outlining the experience, the university name could be dropped in (e.g. 'When attending the lecture at X university, I came across the theory of . . .'). It is not essential to do this; however, if a university sees their name in the personal statement, this can only be a positive as it highlights direct experience and knowledge gained from the university. This helps secure the best fit. The reason, as you'll be aware, that a university cannot be directly mentioned, other than in the strategic way mentioned above, is because only a single personal statement can be submitted and so all five course choices will see the same personal statement and one would not want to alienate another institution.

Compare and take feedback but be balanced

Read multiple personal statement examples – those that are relevant and those that are not relevant to your own course to help generate additional inspiration – whether it be to enhance technique, style or content. It is also important, as I am sure students will do lots of before completing a full draft, to gain as much feedback as possible. What is very important to consider when it comes to feedback are two things in particular: (1) there is reliable feedback and less reliable; (2) opinions vary. When seeking feedback, even if from someone with less knowledge and experience about university education, they may offer an interesting and unique piece of advice that will further enhance the personal statement. However, also keep in mind that ultimately you want the feedback to come from those that have experience in how these should be constructed and have the required ingredients to impress universities. Whether it's about food, art, films, politics and so on, opinions do vary, sometimes rather massively! This is also true with personal statements and so if gaining a lot of advice, keep in mind that some of the feedback may be contradictory. For example, some people may really enjoy a rhetorical question being used in the Question 1 introductory paragraph while others may consider this predictable. It depends. So, as a personal statement writer, stay true to yourself and take in all that you can, with balance, to ensure that you end up with an attention-grabbing personal statement that ticks all the boxes that it needs to but also makes you happy. Afterall, as an applicant, this is your personal statement and your future.

Finally submitting

When you have your final, final draft ready, it is time to put this into the UCAS application before submitting. Some students like to paste their complete draft early into the UCAS portal and then edit from there. My suggestion would be to save multiple drafts in some form of word processing software (e.g. Microsoft Word or Pages) to keep a record and for ease of editing. There will come a time when the final draft will need to be put into the UCAS application which will mostly involve copying and pasting the next.

Character count

As readers of this book will already be aware at this stage, each personal statement question needs to be a minimum of 350 characters and all three questions must add up to a maximum of 4,000 characters. I would recommend maxing out to ensure that all 4,000 characters have been utilised (most personal statements that I have seen total around 3,997 or thereabouts). Not being able to fill all this space suggests either that there is not much there to include or that the applicant has rushed this and is less motivated (both are red flags that should be avoided like the plague). The vast majority of applicants will actually have drafts that are ever so slightly over what's required and so to ensure that there is adequate space (which often is only the difference of eight characters or so) it is very much worth double checking that there are no extra spaces left at the end of full stops at the end of paragraphs or even between words. The UCAS portal picks up on accidental spaces that may be residual remnants of the editing process and so to avoid any unnecessary disappointment of having to delete a few words first check the extra spaces. Another technique that is often used is to close the paragraph spaces between the paragraphs. Generally speaking, this should ideally be avoided as paragraph spaces are a useful and conventional part of writing. Nevertheless, as this is so common and a vestigial of the old personal statement style, with 4,000 characters and 47 lines in a free-flow text, it is conventional in terms of the UCAS world and so can be utilised if needed.

Aside from the personal statement (the overall UCAS application)

In addition to double checking that the personal statement is as well written and effective as possible, do ensure that the overall UCAS application has been filled out correctly (e.g. personal details; contact and residency; education history; course choices). If submitting your personal statement while enrolled at a school and thus having used a buzzword to connect (most likely the vast majority of students reading this), then you should also list someone as a nominated access in your contact section. A nominated access will be able to phone universities and ask questions about the applicant without the applicant being present (due to data protection regulations this is not afforded to those who are not the nominated access). Often students leave this part out and so it is important to consider not ignoring this part of the application if wanting a school staff member to be able to phone/email and ask questions about the application after it has been submitted. Having a nominated access is useful. If an applicant would like a school staff member to contact a university on their behalf who is not a nominated access individual, this can be done by also being present in the phone call and providing verbal permission to discuss the application (or done via email).

After submitting the application, the key is now to ensure that all available time and energy is spent on studying to ensure that the academic conditions of the offer are met or exceeded. Moreover, having great academic results are of course also useful for the future to go in the CV. Some universities also provide merit-based scholarships/financial aid and other incentives if you choose them as the firm choice. Do you research to check if your universities offer this (less do than do not but it is worth double checking nonetheless).

Diversifying your university application portfolio

In addition to focusing on your studies, the other thing that students can do to ensure university success is to diversify their application portfolio. Some UK universities (a very small number) allow for direct applications outside of UCAS. There is Brunel, for instance, which is a popular choice among medics in particular where it is so competitive and other examples that come to mind are UK-based universities that also have campuses overseas (e.g. Northeastern University London, Hult International Business School London and St George's University Grenada). Why not keep your five UCAS choices and increase offers that are on the table by making some direct applications? For direct applications, you can modify your existing personal statement to tailor it to the universities as the personal statement is going directly to them (in this instance it is not considered as self-plagiarism). UCAS also have ways to apply to additional universities (known as Extra and Clearing). Extra is for those who are not holding any offers (either through being unsuccessful in all five original choices or by declining all offers). This is typically open between February and July. UCAS Clearing typically opens from July and places are continuously added around A level Results Day, in August. You can think of UCAS Clearing as a pot that contains all university course places that are still available (either because the course hasn't filled completely or because students have not met the conditions of their offers which has left some places available for others). Clearing is a valuable backup option but has become more than this as students who are holding conditional offers can use this as an opportunity to 'trade up' for more competitive university courses following results day for their pre-university qualifications, especially if they have exceeded their predicted grades. I have seen plenty of Russell Group universities, for example, on Clearing. At the UCAS Conference for Teachers and Advisers 2025, I heard, in a UCAS-led presentation focusing on interesting application data, that the biggest group who used Clearing used to be those who did not secure the grades to meet the conditions of their offer but now this has shifted to those who actively put themselves through Clearing. They do this by declining their university place to find something even more competitive. Interesting data that came from this presentation was that one in 20 applicants went through 'decline my place' to secure their university course and 53% of applicants who declined their place already decided to do so before results day. I still think that Extra and Clearing should be considered as backup options and the mainstream UCAS process should certainly be the emphasis (especially because no one knows which universities will later be using Extra and Clearing).

Reverse admissions

The most exciting way to diversify your application portfolio, in my opinion, is through the concept of reverse admissions. By reversing the application process, students make a profile and universities review these profiles, making a conditional offer (or

5 After Writing

TABLE 14: Three companies that use the concept of reverse admissions.

Name of company	Website	Overview
The Reverse Admissions Portal	www.reverseadmissions.com	A UK-based company specifically supporting international fee-paying students interested in UK universities. Conditional offers are made directly to students as universities review student profiles. No personal statement is needed but applicants will need to upload transcripts of achieved and predicted grades. There may also be an interview request.
Concourse	www.concourse.global	A US-based company that takes a global approach (there are universities listed from many countries), universities review student profiles and make offers to students. There are offers for admission and scholarships. School university counsellors can also leave a reference/note for students that will be read by admissions tutors.
Meto	www.meto-intl.org	Described as an 'online meeting place' for students and universities, Meto takes student information and presents this to universities. If the student information fits with what the university is currently looking for, they may reach out to the student and recommend making an application.

interview request) directly to the student without the student specifically applying. The main company that offers this, in terms of focusing exclusively on UK universities, is known as the Reverse Admissions Portal (although note that this is currently exclusively for university applicants who will be international fee-paying students). There are three main companies in total that offer reverse admissions (as detailed in Table 14). Interestingly, these companies do not require a personal statement. While you have selected five universities through the main process of UCAS, why not expand the available options as a way to increase choice and thus opportunities for university success? These can

TABLE 15: Ways in which applicants can diversify their university course portfolio outside of the five course choices on UCAS.

Method	Where to access	Overview
UCAS Extra	On the UCAS website/UCAS portal	This is for applicants who are not holding any offers (either because all five choices were unsuccessful or the applicant declined all offers). Extra opens after the Equal Consideration Deadline, often available between February and early July, with exact deadlines posted on the UCAS website each year. You can only apply to one university at a time, through Extra. This service is no extra cost.
UCAS Clearing	On the UCAS website/UCAS portal	Typically used after A level results day (or equivalent qualifications), all available university course places are displayed for applicants to choose from. These available places are often due to courses not reaching full capacity or that students who were made conditional offers did not meet the conditions. There are a range of universities available on Clearing, sometimes including a Russell Group. Typically opens in August and ends in September.
Direct applications	See university websites	There are a small number of universities/higher education institutions that may accept applications through UCAS but also allow students to apply directly on their website and sometimes with rolling admissions. This means that students can have more than their five UCAS choices on the go by applying directly. Often these are universities with campuses overseas in addition to a UK base.
Reverse admissions	Reverse Admissions Portal; Concourse; Meto	This also allows students to have more than their five UCAS course choices on the go. Students create a profile on these platforms and universities review these, either contracting students of interest or simply making a conditional offer. There are three main companies which offer this.

all be used in addition to UCAS. Table 15 contains a summary of all the ways applicants can diversify their university course portfolio (expanding on Extra, Clearing, direct applications and reverse admissions).

Finally, it should also be noted that some students diversify their portfolio by applying overseas, often known as the 'UCAS plus' model. In part this is because UK universities can be so competitive and why not therefore open up other opportunities just in case. The other reason might be, especially for international students, because they are unsure on whether to fully commit to studies in the UK or at least because they have the means to study overseas. An overview of how to apply to universities in other countries is beyond the scope of this book but should at least be kept in mind as another way to diversify the application portfolio. A shameless plug that I simply cannot avoid, my next book will be on applying to the US!

Really knowing your personal statement, especially if you might be interviewed

Certainly, university interviews are not an essential part of the application process for the majority of universities and equally interviews are not just reserved for the likes of Oxford and Cambridge. Depending on the course and university, interviews may be part of the application process. Medicine and Dentistry almost always require interviews, often in a multiple mini-interview (MMI) format. Note that university interview requirements may change from year to year, and many universities review interviews on a case-by-case basis, depending on the application pool. It's always a good idea to check each university's website for the most current admissions requirements.

Whether you get asked questions from the content of your personal statement is actually rather unpredictable. For example, I have seen students be interviewed in the same year for the same course and some have been asked specific questions about the personal statement and others less so. While the interview process is designed in a way to try and give applicants an equal chance of receiving an offer the specific way in which an interview is conducted depends heavily on multiple factors, including the interviewer. Either way, just in case, it is essential to ensure that you know your personal statement inside and out in case you are asked a question about this. Know the background of each story you have used, as well as the information surrounding super-curricular activities. Of course, in an interview, this should be an interesting and natural conversation with detail as opposed to short and uncomfortable answers.

The other reason to know your personal statement is, I would say, for a source of inspiration and motivation during the time of your pre-university studies. Completing A levels, for example, can not only be time-consuming but also naturally stressful and so returning back to remind yourself of the next steps of your academic journey is a good way to stay motivated. Strong grades are often a by-product of passion and so the more you remain motivated and academically curious the better your school outcomes will be.

6 Opportunities and challenges of using AI

My initial draft of the contents page did not include this chapter on the use of artificial intelligence, and I was instead simply going to make some overall comments about AI within parts of the book. However, I know that this has been a growing area of interest (or concern!), and after having seen the topic of AI being heavily discussed for two years consecutively, at the UCAS Annual Conference for Teachers and Advisers, I thought that I should actually have a dedicated section. Day One of the 2025 conference took place earlier today, and so after attending the evening activities of an organised drinks reception, dinner and a team quiz, I thought to start this chapter in my hotel room as midnight approaches!

The conference today ended with a plenary session, looking at the UCAS personal statement changes for 2026 and involved a panel discussion and some peer breakout talks. While the focus was on the new personal statements (which, I am happy to confirm, fully corroborated with what has already been mentioned in this book), the topic of AI still made its way into the mix of discussion points. What was clear from this plenary session was that AI is disruptive (it has forced its way as a topic into question) and it is inevitable that we will all have to accept that AI has become part of reality. What is more opaque is understanding what the opportunities of AI for UCAS personal statements are and how AI is presenting unwanted challenges.

The whole point of personal statements, as also reflected in the subtitle of this book, is that they need to be attention-grabbing to get you noticed. Using AI has the potential to remove the individuality element of the writing – in part, because it has not been written by the applicant and also due to the sometimes unnatural or robotic style that AI can sometimes bring. From the personal statement examples that I have seen, generated with heavy use of AI, they appear extremely cliché, lack structure, good writing flow and use of genuine anecdotes. However, I do think AI in personal statement writing is nuanced, and there are certainly benefits. I wouldn't, by any means, encourage or suggest that students have to use AI for their personal statements. Nevertheless, I can appreciate the opportunities that it offers and so will leave this as optional. What we should amplify from the outset, very distinctively, is that there is a difference between cheating by using AI to simply write something for you vs. the action of using AI to generate ideas, and this brainstorming usage is ultimately what I am referring to when stating that there are opportunities, and in this context, the decision of whether or not to use AI is optional. Of course, an AI-generated personal statement should not be directly copied and pasted.

UCAS does, famously, use software to check for similarities in personal statements and so does have measures in place to tackle personal statements that have been copied. At the time of writing, I have been informed by UCAS that they do not employ AI detection software and so do not overtly ban or even discourage the use of AI. While this does not stop universities using AI detection themselves, I have not heard of any cases where they do, and a significant reason for this is due to the current uncertainty about AI use plus the high rate of false positives found with AI detection. I have found one case of a university colour coding based on AI detection, but this was only used as a mild indication and did not feature in the final decision process of whether to admit students. Such as AI itself, the topic of AI in personal statements and even in education more generally is fast evolving, and so we will all need to watch this space. My current feeling is that AI will continue to be embraced, albeit there will be more clarity on what is acceptable and unacceptable usage, or at least there will be greater guidance on best practices. What we can take away is that as long as there is no direct plagiarism or other infringements on policies, AI can be used.

If properly utilised, the main benefits that come to mind for the use of AI in personal statements are initial brainstorming; generating content ideas; structuring and formatting; editing and proofreading. Therefore, it is possible to acknowledge that ChatGPT and other AI tools have the potential to enhance personal statements and offer support for applicants who may find this valuable. In the same way that a student may ask a teacher or family member for advice on what they should study or what sort of skills they should highlight to enhance their competitiveness for a particular university course, AI can also provide some very interesting answers. Simply asking ChatGPT, for example, 'What are some relevant super-curricular activities when applying for a degree in Computer Science?' can offer some suggestions and provide a comprehensive starting point. This question, as well as many others that one may have about personal statements, could be put to AI. There are other AI-powered tools that can support the writing process, such as a platform known as Jenni, that looks at grammar, style and readability. When you highlight text within Jenni, there are certain commands (e.g. 'improve fluency', 'paraphrase' or 'simplify'). You, as the writer, will identify what in your written text could be modified. Maybe, for example, you think that a section of a paragraph about a work experience is too waffly and you'd like to reduce this to save some characters. I don't actually see much of a difference between asking AI for suggestions vs. a teacher or university counsellor reading a personal statement and annotating it with some recommended changes.

If a student is using a personal statement template from their school, in terms of giving themselves an unfair advantage, what is the difference in asking AI for a suggested personal statement structure? In fact, using AI independently does show initiative rather than relying on resources handed to them. Another reason that AI is beneficial is that UCAS and many universities have placed significant emphasis on widening participation and access for potentially disadvantaged groups (including lowering academic entry requirements). Well, having the ability to use AI, it could be argued, levels the playing field in terms of enabling any applicant with an internet connection to have their own mentor and tutor (especially if their school does not have a skilled careers adviser or dedicated university counsellor). AI, in this sense, equalises opportunity. If you, as a student, direct AI, for example, to suggest ways in which your personal statement could be more persuasive, it is still you who has identified that there needs to be more persuasiveness in your personal statement and so, in effect, you are still demonstrating the required writing skills whether or not you used AI in the first place. The key, however, is to use AI for inspiration and suggestions but still ultimately to use your own words as opposed to copying and pasting.

The use of AI is extremely uncertain in this current climate of a disruptive force without universally accepted parameters for best practice. What is unanimous, however, with the many universities I have talked to about this, is that they would like to ensure an 'ethical usage of AI'. This is essential. AI use should not be a modern synonym for plagiarism. You need to write your own personal statement but have the option of considering utilising AI. Artificial intelligence is changing many sectors and ironically, I have heard that even a small number of universities are starting to consider employing AI in their own admissions processes as a way of assessing applicants. It is very early and in its infancy, but shows AI's versatility and how permeable it is to many aspects of our daily lives. It would be beyond the scope of this section to walk you through how to navigate AI-powered tools. The main point here is to offer some dialogue and information on how AI could be used. I think AI can be used for personal statements but is absolutely not essential. I should also note that just because AI is a source of answering questions in real-time, it doesn't necessarily mean that AI will save time or offer better answers that could come from elsewhere. Keep this in mind and be strategic, as well as ethical, should you choose to use AI in the personal statement process. Table 16 provides an overview of some evaluative points, showing some of the opportunities but also current challenges in using AI in the development of personal statements.

TABLE 16: Opportunities and challenges of AI for personal statement writing.

Opportunities	Challenges
Can be used to generate ideas and brainstorm (just like asking a teacher, friend or family member a question).	There is a risk of overusing this or falling into the trap of falsifying the personal statement by completely having AI write the entire personal statement.
Offers a way of rewriting sentences into interesting and meaningful prose (an enhancement tool but not that dissimilar from spell checks and grammar checks and thesauruses that have been used for many years).	There is a risk of AI 'hallucinating' and if not picked up can lead to false, misleading or otherwise inaccurate text therefore negatively impacting the quality (and success) of the personal statement.
At the time of writing, UCAS do not use AI detection software (only similarity reports) and so they are not explicitly monitoring this or overtly banning the utilisation of AI in helping to create personal statements.	Universities are able to assess personal statements however they choose and so it is unclear if they will use their own AI detection and whether this has a negative impact on the student's application.
AI has taken the world by storm and has been adopted by many industries and companies. There are multiple research and writing tools that harness this technology.	AI is extremely new and still developing. There is uncertainty about how it could be best used and regulated. Therefore, users of AI have to be cautious.

7 Personal statement examples

There are few resources or pieces of advice that are more useful to prepare for writing an attention-grabbing UCAS personal statement than actually reading some model examples. Here, we have six examples from different subject areas. Whatever the university course, naturally, reading these personal statements will still be useful to offer you some tangible sense of style, structure, uniqueness and use of super-curricular activities. Pay less attention to whether this course matches your own preferred university course if you are a student reading this, and focus more on how these examples can help shape and refine your own approach. At the time of writing, we are about to go into the first use of the next format that UCAS is launching (exciting times!). As such, there are no model examples to be found. Therefore, I have actually consulted three of my long-standing colleagues, and even better friends, to help write some excellent personal statement examples based on the advice found in this book. A huge thank you must go to Dr Dan Casey, Dr Elizabeth Mackintosh and Dr Clodomiro Cafolla for providing these model personal statements. Much of the content is based on true life events. For one of these personal statement examples, Dan interestingly used his original UCAS personal statement that he submitted for his degree in Geography (he studied at the University of Cambridge) as a basis and then updated and refined it for the present day and new format based on the approach of this book. As I understand that readers of this book will come from a range of academic backgrounds and countries, I have tried to incorporate a range of pre-university qualifications in these model examples (A levels, International Baccalaureate and Italy's Liceo Classico are represented). I have written commentaries for each personal statement.

7 Personal Statement Examples

Example 1: Geography

Question 1: *Why do you want to study this course or subject?*

Geography is unique in breadth and ability to span the natural and social sciences. As Richard Burton said 'If geography itself has any significance it is that we are made to lift our eyes from ourselves to the whole complex and magnificent world'. My interest ignited through Geography coming alive in the news. For instance, last summer, Southern Europe experienced heatwaves with temperatures exceeding 45°C, compounded by El Niño, which intensified weather patterns. This led to wildfires, tourists being stranded, and the cancellation of flights, having extreme environmental and economic impacts.

Given my environmental interest the book most intriguing for me was Lovelock's 'The revenge of Gaia'. The Gaia hypothesis in the 1970s of a living Earth – one where humans are part of a system, was a revolutionary idea, yet rejected by many until recently. I also found it refreshing to read another viewpoint on combating climate change, one where sustainable development is too late and where we now must prepare through sustainable retreat and geo-engineering. Although some optimism and potential solutions are possible. At the inaugural session of my school's Geography society, I recall a discussion on Dorling's Population 10 Billion. I found his criticism of the carbon trading system convincing, which I later found to be supported by an LSE study that showed Dorling's push for a progressive tax system could minimise environmental costs without restricting growth. His method, I argue, provides an effective way to rein in carbon emissions, and a hybrid model consisting of a cap on emissions and a price ceiling for carbon permits may be the best remedy. Such initiatives help mitigate the long-term effects climate change has, moving towards achieving a sustainable global economy. It is Geography's positioning at the intersection of subjects and its potential to solve such challenges which appeals to me.

I believe I have the skills a Geographer needs. I hope later to pursue postgraduate study, always having a desire to learn and gain new experiences, whether exploring new cultures or travelling.

2,116 characters

Question 2: *How have your qualifications and studies helped you to prepare for this course or subject?*

Throughout Geography A-Level I have enjoyed modules on geopolitics and technological innovation to combat environmental issues, complementing my Economics study. I was interested in how the USA has allies to use as 'buffer states' and how politically it can influence any company or country. Studying French has enhanced my communication and essay writing. Learning about a different culture has also furthered my understanding about how geographical environments can influence the history of citizens living there. Over the last two years I self-taught

AS Level Geology and currently taking exams. This furthered my scientific knowledge of geological events and hazards, which I took as I believed it to be relevant and closely related to geomorphology courses at university.

I attended the LSE Choice Geography summer school and sixteen Saturday sessions, advancing my knowledge and preparing me further for university, alongside being a Royal Geographical Society member and regularly attending lectures. Last summer I volunteered on the Earthwatch project 'Climate Change At The Arctic's Edge'. The research examined the impact climate change was having on wetland ecosystems surrounding Churchill, Canada, specifically monitoring boreal and wood frogs alongside stickleback fish. I analysed the water quality and physical features of wetlands. I had to adapt quickly, with conditions vulnerable to change and arduous fieldwork and lab work, advancing my research capabilities.

1,480 characters

Question 3: *What else have you done to prepare outside of education, and why are these experiences useful?*

Beyond the classroom I aid my community, as an intergenerational volunteer for Age Concern. I am an altar server at my church and have led citizenship to year seven pupils weekly. I have also joined the Alternative Choir at school. This taught me about different generational perspectives, worldwide current affairs, and enabled me to learn more about society, feeding into wider university life.

396 characters

TOTAL: 3,992 characters

Commentary on Example 1

Question 1

The personal statement opens with an interesting hook. In this example, there is a short sentence that highlights subject passion and knowledge about the breadth of the subject of geography. In order for the applicant to make such a claim about geography's interdisciplinary nature, the applicant will have had to delve into the subject, and thus this showcases subject passion and knowledge. Moreover, such a comment about the subject is a way to grab the attention of the reader. In addition, as the very first sentence of the whole personal statement, it was very good to see that the course itself (Geography) was named from the outset. Sometimes, applicants may go through a whole paragraph without mentioning the course name, and therefore it is left up to the admissions tutor to ascertain subject suitability. To mention the course early on is a subtle way to inform the reader that this is a very specific personal statement tailored to the right course. It is not always the case that a quotation has to be used, and, in fact, often using a quotation is considered cliché (even more so if the quote is at the very beginning). Instead, rather powerfully, the applicant has used a quotation to further demonstrate the initial opening point about the unique qualities of geography's ability to span natural and social sciences. Be cautious of overly using quotations, but in this example, the quotation was effective. A tremendous way to connect with the reader and to be extremely unique (and thus memorable) is to discuss a specific crystallising moment – when exactly did you realise that this subject is what you want to pursue for the next few years of your life? The applicant here gave the example of the news and provided a specific news story. A crystallising moment doesn't have to be a news story; there are many other possibilities. For instance: something from a lecture, podcast, relevant project or personal life experience and so on.

The applicant here is using this personal statement in an effective way to sell their unique qualities and subject interests. In this example, an interest in the environment. A useful sentence starter was 'Given my environmental interest . . .' This is a fantastic way to not only immediately inform the reader that you have developed specific academic curiosity around the subject but to also then offer a segue into discussing relevant super-curricular activities. The applicant here chose to bring in some wider reading. It is important to have some use of key terminology and detailed academic knowledge. In this example, we see the inclusion of relevant theory (The Gaia hypothesis). The applicant is not just naming relevant subject content but is providing a deeper (albeit very brief) reflection – '. . . a revolutionary idea, yet rejected by many until recently'. It is a valuable technique to not necessarily develop a full academic argument or debate, but to offer some critique to show the ability to evaluate topics within the field. The applicant does this here by contrasting: 'I also found it refreshing to read another viewpoint on combating climate change . . .' A useful approach to showcase academic passion for your chosen course is to show how one experience leads to another – that is, how one super-curricular exposure ignites your curiosity to learn more. We can see it happening in this personal statement where the applicant comments on Dorling's Population 10 Billion and follows up on an interesting criticism with wider reading (an LSE study). The applicant then goes on to provide his opinions on Dorling's method. It is not necessarily easy to engage with the field by developing some form of evaluative overtones, and if done correctly, admissions tutors have informed me that a display of such interest and command of the subject is a fantastic way to be further noticed and positively scored.

We can see that the applicant has spent a tremendous amount of time refining this personal statement and thinking deeply about the structure and qualities he wants to convey to the reader. For example, when first opening with the comment about the interdisciplinary nature of geography, the applicant then returns to this comment towards the end of Question 1: 'It is Geography's positioning at the intersection of subjects and its potential to solve such challenges which appeals to me.' Think about your desired themes that you would want to present in your personal statement and consider returning to these once or twice to enhance structure and continuity for the reader – hit home with your messaging. Moreover, the applicant has clearly identified reasons for why he's so interested in the subject and did not shy away from clarifying this. Readers here can see that the applicant is deeply passionate about geography. He then closes Question 1 by detailing plans for the future (continuing with postgraduate study). Stating your future plans is not essential, but can offer a valid reason for your interest in pursuing such a course.

Question 2

This can be a particularly difficult question – on the one hand, students really should not be listing their current subjects or describing all the topics covered; on the other hand, this is also a very new question and so can be challenging for school staff/ university counsellors to make tangible suggestions of what to include as, at least if reading this book in 2025, they will not have previous examples to go by. The other two UCAS questions are very much the usual bread and butter of what has always been expected – why do you want to study the course and what have you done outside of the classroom to prepare? To specifically draw upon your classroom subject and wider studies may have formed personal statement content selected by applicants in the past, but this was by no means essential. So, I hope this book and the model personal statements within may be of some inspiration! Here, we can see that the applicant has divided their answer into two parts. The first part specifically goes to the A levels being studied, but rather than needlessly listing subject content, there is a deeper introspection about some exact topics within the subjects and how this links to his academic interests. Isolating topics (e.g. geopolitics and the environment) served as a platform to then demonstrate a wider understanding of relevant knowledge for Geography, in this case, the existence of buffer states. The applicant has been effective in considering how his current studies may have developed other relevant skills — for example, cultural understanding through studying a language. As you know, writing a personal statement is very much about selling yourself, and therefore use any opportunities you identify to be your biggest cheerleader. The applicant was successful in doing so by using this section as an opportunity to highlight something interesting about his self-motivation and academic ability (self-teaching AS level Geology). This is absolutely not a blanket endorsement for encouraging mass self-studying of an AS level but simply a demonstration of how this section can be used to bring your unique academic experiences to the attention of the reader. Each individual will likely have their own unique experiences and resulting attributes.

The applicant didn't just stop there. The second section of this answer was used to amplify the engagement with other super-curricular activities, especially those which are project and studies-based to fit in with the Question 2 UCAS personal statement. You may be thinking why some of this content, with such a super-curricular nature, is not in Question 1. This reminds me of a conversation with a student recruitment representative from the University of Cambridge last January: even though there are multiple questions/sections (three) that make up the personal statement, the personal statement will often still be read as one single document. In other words, while the updated structure imposes dedicated sections, the content of what you want to include will be considered by the reader in its totality and so I would recommend spending less time worrying about where to include content and more time ensuring that you have covered all that you want to include (with slightly less focus on where you fit it in). This section provided a decent number of super-curricular activities – a summer school, membership in an academic institution, lecture attendance, relevant volunteering and engagement in research. Remember, while this is a Geography personal statement, you can see that no matter the subject focus, you can extract ideas for useful super-curricular activities. For instance, in this case it was the Royal Geographical Society, but it could have been the academic institution of the Royal College of Surgeons of Edinburgh, Royal Institute of British Architects or the British Psychological Society. While the applicant could have perhaps included lesser listing of experiences and more expansion with deeper academic reflection from his experiences (a suggestion of an alternative approach here), he was nonetheless masterful in selecting super-curricular activities and expanding on these to showcase academic passion, curiosity and thus suitability for the course. Note how subtle hints were included (e.g. 'preparing me further for university'). I also liked how the applicant was able to extrapolate key ways in which he has academically developed: 'I had to adapt quickly, with conditions vulnerable to change and arduous fieldwork and lab work, advancing my research capabilities.' Feel free to be explicit and overt in stating relevant skills, qualities and attributes.

Question 3

Looking back to the now-called 'old' personal statements, it will be particularly useful for career advisers and university counsellors to think about the third question here as similar to the penultimate paragraph/section at the bottom of the old personal statement, which involved a nod to some extra-curricular content. In this third question, universities are looking for evidence that the student is engaged in wider non-academic activities and thus is a rounded individual who is able to contribute to wider university life. It is not only about suitability for the academic course applied to but also an indication that the applicant has what it takes to enjoy their time and enhance the social fabric of the institution. Competitive universities, in particular, look for more super-curricular than extra-curricular activities and, therefore, as a rule of thumb, I would recommend devoting less space to this question than to the other two. In this example, we can see that the applicant has drawn on his volunteering experiences and his participation in church/music activities – this offers the reader a deeper glimpse into his personal life and therefore provides an opportunity to connect with the applicant and gain an appreciation for possible ways that the applicant could flourish in a university context. What was particularly effective in this answer was that the applicant was explicit in identifying qualities and skills enhanced through these activities outside of education (e.g. knowledge of current affairs). This is a strategic way to bridge the utility in such qualities useful for wider life but also link back to the university course.

Example 2: Medicine

Question 1: *Why do you want to study this course or subject?*

With my mum dying from multiple myeloma I reflected on the care by the NHS, the relationships with fellow patients on wards; creating community, and the dignity staff afforded her. A difficult moment in life but a turning point, I understood my calling as a doctor. I seek to be compassionate and empathetic, someone able to advance the frontiers of knowledge, providing patients the best chance of survival.

I wanted to learn more about my mum's case, so I read Cowan et al.'s 'Diagnosis and Management of Multiple Myeloma'. It explained the disease cause as abnormal clonal plasma cells in the bone marrow, with chance of uncontrollable spread, resulting in medical complications like anaemia, hypercalcemia, and kidney damage. The paper explained treatments start to control gradually transitioning to maintenance; induction therapy followed by treatment with autologous hematopoietic stem cell transplantation, and maintenance therapy with lenalidomide. Advancement in stem cell therapy was particularly novel for me and so I read 'Advancements in the Treatment of Multiple Myeloma' by Zavaleta-Monestel et al. The significance was that while no cure exists hope pertains for managing the condition, extending life expectancy, and increasing quality of life.

To hone my skills I worked in oncology at Chelsea and Westminster. I shadowed a consultant, who delivered a stage 2 lung cancer diagnosis, following a biopsy and PET scan. The doctor built rapport, asking his family to wait outside, ensuring confidentiality, before taking a seat and asking questions about his day. The doctor then reassured him but in clear jargon explained what lung cancer was, survival rates, and chemotherapy treatment plans. The patient was understandably concerned and teary. The doctor ensured his understanding before leaving, also offering tea. This signified the importance of interpersonal skills, empathy, and communication within Medicine. Thus, I read a book by Gawande, Being Mortal. It was a pessimistic take on what doctors failed to do but how the ultimate goal for doctors should be to encourage a good life, not a good death. This resonated with me having also worked at the John Radcliffe in A&E, observing numerous cases admitted, all with doctors focused on saving lives and providing sound discharge advice. Traditionally, while Medicine may be associated with death, I now consider it as the art of life.

2,410 characters

Question 2: *How have your qualifications and studies helped you to prepare for this course or subject?*

Studying English B HL, I learnt the art of communication, importance of argument construction, and need for thought clarity. Understanding that we live in a globalised world I also chose Spanish SL, as communicating with patients who may not speak English is fundamental. To further my scientific reasoning and lab skills I undertook HL Chemistry and Biology courses, obtaining a Silver Award in the Cambridge Chemistry Challenge. I studied Geography SL to learn more about global affairs and distribution of diseases globally. With numeracy key to ensure drugs are dispensed correctly and research data analysed appropriately I also took Mathematics: analysis and approaches. For my Biology extended essay I examined the role of cardiovascular disease spread among developed and less developed nations, combining an interest in Geography to explore how risk factors change.

At my school I participate in Med Soc, discussing NHS hot topics, ethics, and hearing from guest speakers. This enthralled me given contemporary topical issues like antibiotic resistance, while enhancing my debating skills. I also engaged in virtual experiences with Medic Mentor and Future Learn, gaining insights into diseases and medical skills.

1,223 characters

Question 3: *What else have you done to prepare outside of education, and why are these experiences useful?*

Beyond school I volunteer in Oxfam, and also have been a keen gymnast at my local club. This enabled me to engage with members of the public from diverse backgrounds, help others, and also maintain a work-life balance. I also enjoy knitting gifts for my family, to enhance my manual dexterity. I read novels to expand my vocabulary and further my English.

355 characters

TOTAL: 3,988 characters

Commentary on Example 2

Question 1

Having read an extremely large number of UCAS personal statements over the years, I am constantly impressed and humbled by the myriad of personal anecdotes that applicants share. Personal anecdotes are, by far, the best way to connect with the reader (e.g. admissions tutor) and therefore they increase your chances of being unique and memorable. Separate yourself from the competition! The applicant here has used a very personal and emotive moment where it was confirmed that the university course (in this case Medicine) is the correct calling. Surprisingly, I have rarely (if ever) seen a personal anecdote be the same. Think deeply about that crystallising moment when you realised that this course was the right choice for you and write from the heart. Going straight to your crystallising moment, in the first personal statement question, is a great method to protect yourself from being drawn to use cliché quotations, statistics and references to key people in the industry (e.g. referring to Elon Musk for an Engineering personal statement). What is clear to all is that each student is eligible for more than one type of course at university – that is, your school subject choices, grades and experiences render you an applicant who has multiple options at their disposal. Consequently, it is extremely important to inform the reader as to exactly why you have selected this university course over so many other ones. For instance, in this example, why Medicine and not a degree in Cell Biology, Biochemistry, Biomedical Sciences or Public Health? Often prospective medical students fall into seemingly difficult-to-avoid clichés, such as stating that they want to help people and see their calling as one of service. Universities want to see more. In particular, that you are deeply fascinated by the underpinning science within Medicine. The applicant here could have delved deeper into the biology within the introduction but at stated one of the reasons for undertaking this degree as 'advancing the frontiers of knowledge' and so ticked the box of avoiding purely wanting to help others. Think about common clichés of motivational reasons for your own university course choices and ensure that you avoid these and go deeper into why you would like to dedicate at least the next three years of your life to university study.

In the next paragraph of Question 1, the applicant goes into more research and highlights subject knowledge by referencing some interesting academic papers and enhancing this paragraph by reflecting on what has been read. An essential feature of successful personal statements is that they go well beyond merely describing but also offer some evaluation, critical analysis and measured reflection. Following the outlining of the content of one paper, the applicant then wrote: 'Advancement in stem cell therapy was particularly novel for me and so I read . . .'. Identifying areas of interest and then using these as a springboard for further super-curricular exploration (in this case, with relevant wider reading) is a great technique to segue between experiences and reflections. The applicant commented that while there is no found cure as of yet, there is progress in other forms of deliverable patient outcomes (useful reflection). What also stood out in this section was the use of relevant key terminology (e.g. 'autologous hematopoietic stem cell transplantation'). This is also important – do write with a style that is accessible to all readers but also keep in mind that your personal statement should be tailored to readers who have some knowledge of your course. Some universities have non-subject-specific readers who are the first round of admissions tutors, who retain the stronger personal statements ready for academic department readers. Others only use academic readers, and other universities only have non-specific ones. Either way, including some detailed understanding of your course is an advantageous way to ensure that you amplify your demonstration of knowledge and passion for your field – no matter the specific academic level of the reader. Cover yourself for all eventualities by striking a balance which is understandable for all but also ultimately academically interesting.

As for all courses offered at university, they require applicants to not only have subject passion and curiosity but also an enhanced set of skills relevant to succeed within the field. In this case, the applicant identified some useful skills worth highlighting to include interpersonal skills, empathy and communication. To guide the reader, you could include some of what I call 'setup sentence starters'. Specifically, they explicitly inform the reader what you are about to do and therefore they prime the reader. For example, in the final paragraph of Question 1, you can see the applicant starts this by writing: 'To hone my skills . . .'. Some admissions tutors have specific guidelines that they use when analysing a personal statement; others do not have a formal list of things to look out for in the personal statement but informally have a specific list in their minds which they refer to when scanning through. Either way, using these setup sentence starters ensures that the reader metaphorically or literally ticks off key requirements as they analyse the personal statement. These requirements/guidelines vary but essentially include all that we have covered in this book (including subject passion; relevant super-curricular activities; demonstration of relevant skills, etc.). The applicant drew upon a range of super-curricular activities and used one to inform the other (e.g. wanting to read a related book after shadowing a doctor). Finally, although it is not easy to do but very effective when wanting to remain original and thus memorable, if you can include one or two unique and insightful soundbites to amplify your knowledge and consideration of the field as a whole, this elevates the quality of the personal statement. The nice soundbite (almost like a non-cliché bumper sticker) used here can be seen in the final sentence: 'Traditionally, whilst Medicine may be associated with death, I now consider it as the art of life.'

Question 2

Here we have the example of a student taking the International Baccalaureate, as opposed to A levels (most of our examples). It perhaps goes without saying – Question 2 (as well as the entirety of your personal statement) is tailored to your specific context. So, whether you are completing the IB, A levels, or another set of pre-university studies, understand your niche and then market yourself! As you can see in this example of a Question 2 answer, the applicant has not simply listed a range of school subjects but has selectively identified relevant academic experiences and successfully amplified the benefit of undertaking these in relation to preparing for the university course at hand. Remember, the admissions tutors will already know which pre-university studies you are taking – this is listed in the education section of your UCAS application – consequently, use your character space wisely.

A useful technique is to either start with the relevant skill developed or end the sentence with a reflection on how this experience has prepared you for the university studies you hope to embark on. Using a combination of top and bottom-ended sentences creates some variety in your writing, which makes it more interesting and thus readable. The applicant has used a combination. For instance, starting with 'To further my scientific reasoning and lab skills I . . .' or ending with 'as communicating with patients who may not speak English is fundamental'. Consider using this technique. You do not have too many characters available (only 4,000 total!). Rather than having the reader infer your skills, qualities and suitability for the course you're applying to make the reader's job even easier by showcasing these in the open.

As I would recommend for a Question 2 part of the personal statement, you do not need to only point to your school studies and identify the skills developed, but also discuss some of your other studies outside of the classroom. Here, the applicant had a final paragraph linking in relevant academic experiences, namely super-curricular activities. These included a school society and an online course. Again, whatever the course area at university, you could take some inspiration from both the structure and overall deployment of relevant experiences to enhance your own personal statement (or guidance as a university counsellor). There is somewhat of an occasional blur in whether some super-curricular activities should be included in Question 1 or Question 2. You can always have multiple drafts and see what works best in terms of fitting in with your paragraph topics/themes. As mentioned before, the personal statement will in fact be read in its entirety, and so it is less important where you put the content and more so that you have included all that you want.

Question 3

Even though extra-curricular activities often point to your wider skills and non-academic roundedness as a candidate, don't feel as if you cannot use these to again magnify your suitability for your chosen university course. Medicine offers a fantastic example of how non-academic pursuits (e.g. knitting) can be linked to relevant skills required for the course (e.g. manual dexterity for surgical procedures). Whether you are applying to Medicine specifically, think of other relevant subject-specific qualities that you can subtly lean on. Examples may include (but are not limited to): communication skills; leadership; analytical thinking; an awareness of current affairs; attention to detail. All of these (and many more!) can be demonstrated through extra-curricular activities.

Example 3: Economics

Question 1: *Why do you want to study this course or subject?*

Being raised in Bangkok's gold trade, my curiosity in Economics grew. Through my parents' gold shop I pondered gold's high commodity value. Growing up in the shop, I surveyed customers' behaviour and the nature of the business. I questioned gold's distinctive characteristics of rarity, durability, cultural significance, and economic utility. I soon realised its investment appeal as a liquid entity and something able to withstand inflation and recession.

With my interest in the financial world, I questioned the past importance of gold. I examined the 1997 Asian Financial Crisis. I sought to understand how the Financial Crisis could have been prevented, creating a timeline of gold; I noticed the countries facing the worst of the crisis all lacked gold reserves. Historically, physical gold had little credit risk and was an asset outperforming others. Hypothetically, if these Asian countries reserved gold rather than foreign currencies, the aftermath perhaps could be less critical. I further researched this cataclysm, reading articles from the Economist and a paper entitled 'Thailand's Monetary Policy Since the 1997 Crisis' by Nakornthob, and never thought that when the Thai government floated the Baht it would cause a chain reaction triggering the region's downfall.

My rumination of such world crises led me to read Taleb's 'The Black Swan'. A black swan event being one of rarity, extreme impact, and retrospective predictability. Taleb argued that many current models are outdated and lack robustness to predict such events, particularly with his explanation of survivorship bias through Wald's American aircraft armour anecdote. I believe tackling and preventing economic turmoil should come with precautions. Global issues cannot be solved using past solutions. Regardless of how similar an event is historically, we humans typically ignore little details and are careless to reach conclusions, as evidenced in duplicable situations like the 'Dot-Com' Bubble.

From a childhood interest to a fundamental part of my current studies, Economics illustrates and solves society's greatest challenges. I see Economics as a pathway to my ambition of investment banking.

2,180 characters

Question 2: *How have your qualifications and studies helped you to prepare for this course or subject?*

A Level Physics taught me to think logically in a process-driven way, undertaking Isaac Physics challenges and receiving a Gold in the Physics Olympiad. My team also won the Space Design Competition, where I calculated the costs of production of a new space settlement and most efficient resource allocation, linking to my Economics interest. Maths allowed me to refine my abstract reasoning skills, and I achieved a Silver in the UKMT Senior Challenge. Prior to my A Levels, I also maintained a keen interest in these subjects, earning a gold and 'Best in School' in the UKMT Junior Challenge 2 years in a row. I also was awarded Gold awards yearly in the PAMA mental maths competitions, illustrating my ability to solve problems quickly.

Partaking in the NCH London Essay Competition 2025 I received 'Highly Commended'. The task was to analyse possible impacts of Russian economic sanctions. I researched data and views from various sites and employed A Level Economics knowledge to examine impacts across these regions: South America, Europe, Asia, and Russia. I argued that Europe was most likely to see the worst impacts, given their overdependence on Russian gas and that many countries are part of the EU tradebloc which condone Russia's actions, while alternative nations remain more neutral. This experience taught me about citing and enhanced my analytical skills.

1,374 characters

Question 3: *What else have you done to prepare outside of education, and why are these experiences useful?*

I enjoy language learning, currently practicing Mandarin, reaching HSK 3 level, a skill particularly useful in a globalised world where economics knows no bounds. I am a player for my local club's football team, earning the sportsmanship award. Moreover, I enjoy music, improvising songs on the piano, while also teaching myself the guitar. This shows my holistic development and willingness to contribute to all aspects of university life.

441 characters

TOTAL: 3,995 characters

Commentary on Example 3

Question 1

Immediately, from the outset, we get a snippet of the personal background of the applicant – someone exposed to the gold trade in Bangkok through the family business. This allows the reader to connect with the applicant and provides a unique context to remember this personal statement and set it apart from others. The applicant identified the commodity of gold as a particular area of interest and turned this into a running theme throughout the piece. While it is not always essential to have a specific topic running throughout the personal statement, doing so in an effective way can be an interesting method of providing a unique piece of writing. I have seen other running themes in the past, such as a focus on the superhero Iron Man for an Engineering personal statement (which was successful). The key is that, if students do decide to go down this path, they must ensure that the personal statement is still varied in terms of super-curricular activities, and the theme can be referred to throughout, but there has to be a balance to avoid making this theme too overpowering. The applicant has done well to find a great balance here of discussing gold while also bringing in a plethora of relevant experiences and knowledge to supplement.

What's also clear is that this is a personal statement aimed at Economics. A good technique is to mention the specific course early within the introductory paragraph. This helps the reader know that you are passionate and have relevant experiences directed to a specific course that is offered at the university. There is also, in the introduction, the inclusion of relevant key terminology ('liquid entity'; 'inflation and recession'). This helps to build and maintain an overall academic overtone. (As well as demonstrating your knowledge.)

Moving on to the second paragraph, we can see a great example of a setup sentence starter: 'With my interest in the financial world . . .' This is an extremely vivid way to showcase a sense of subject passion and curiosity – overtly highlighting an interest from the beginning. Demonstrating knowledge of the course, we can see some inclusion of relevant information, such as in this example, the use of a case study (the 1997 Asian Financial Crisis). While trying to avoid being too cliché, consider identifying a monumental moment/theory/theorist to keep the reader not only entertained by eagerly waiting to read more about your reflection or critical analysis of the topic but also nodding along under the view of considering the applicant as someone who has extensively studied the university course they're applying for. Another method to signify extensive studying and an early mastery of your course is to create an opportunity of being able to interject a sentence or two containing objective information relevant to the course. We can see an example of this when the applicant wrote: 'Historically, physical gold had little credit risk and was an asset outperforming others.' This clear, concise and possibly even authoritative snippet of information is a subtle but powerful way of amplifying the impression that you have read around the field. In other words, while you have not yet been to university, you still possess some background knowledge and thus the ability to contribute in seminar/lecture theatre discussions.

Finally, as mentioned in the commentary I gave on personal statement example 2, the icing on the cake can come in the form of a soundbite. While on occasion they can be cliché, such comments can also be unique and thought-provoking. This is probably one of the very few (if not the only) moments where I would consider being somewhat cliché as acceptable. Have you been able to already identify the soundbite? Here it is: 'Global issues cannot be solved using past solutions.' Very nice. It is also rather nice – not essential, but worth considering – to end Question 1 with a short mini-conclusion. It's almost like a continuation from the introduction, completing the missing part with a rounding off of why this has to be the course to study at university. It helps to establish a succinct and coherent structure.

Question 2

At first glance, on the surface level, physics may not be the first subject that comes to mind when considering preparation for undertaking a degree in Economics. Nevertheless, the applicant has done very well to change minds and, moreover, very effectively demonstrate the transferable benefits. Namely, these benefits are identified as enabling one to ' . . . think logically in a process-driven way . . .' In addition, mentioning a subject is a perfect chance to also embed some related awards and achievements. In this case, the award is an impressive Gold in the Physics Olympiad. Again, the Space Design Competition may not innately be a concrete demonstration of preparedness for Economics, but yet again the applicant was able to identify extremely tangible experiences. Here, the applicant wrote about calculating costs and resource allocation. This shows the reader that no matter the subject, the applicant can excel (e.g. the Gold Award) and also find ways to bring this back to the main course passion – in this case, Economics.

Mathematics is perhaps an easier subject to link with Economics. The applicant, again, rather skilfully, does not just list or describe what was learned at school for Mathematics but uses this question as a platform to best engage in some self-marketing – detailing relevant academic competitions. Depending on your own experiences, the self-marketing does not have to necessarily contain academic competitions. The linking, in fact, could be any relevant super-curricular activity that fits in well. As we see at the end of this paragraph, the applicant went one step further to actually identify a specific skill obtained through engagement with their school subject: '. . . illustrating my ability to solve problems quickly'. Consider which skills and qualities you would like to tease out as you also engage in some reflection and self-marketing!

As we can see here, as well as in other examples, Question 2 does not just have to contain classroom subjects. For instance, the applicant referred to participating in an essay competition and then linked A level Economics before sharing a critical analysis of the essay topic at hand. While a personal statement is not an academic essay as such, do not feel that you cannot incorporate one or two evaluative points which have the effect of reinforcing the message to the reader that you have engaged in a large amount of research which has relevance for your chosen course. If you make some academic reflections, about current affairs, for instance, this is a wonderful way to render your personal statement not just an informative but also an entertaining read for the admissions tutor.

Question 3

This question looks for evidence of an applicant's character and engagement with interesting, often non-academic activities, rendering him or her into a rounded candidate. In a relatively small number of characters, less than 500, the applicant was successful in showcasing three activities (language learning, sports and music). Moreover, there was not just a listing and brief description, but a very effective use of words to engage in some self-marketing. What was particularly effective was the way the applicant brought this back to the university degree (Economics), even though this was not necessarily about academic pursuits. (An impressive way to clearly show the reader that you are passionate about the course you're applying to.) Football, in this example, led to a tangible outcome of earning a sportsmanship award, and music offered a chance to highlight dedication, motivation and independence – being self-taught on the guitar! The final sentence was particularly effective – while at times being subtle is also effective and we should see some of that, also don't hold back on being explicit. Make the job easy for the reader to know that you have plenty of desirable attributes rather than them having to tease this out. The final sentence was direct: 'This shows my holistic development and willingness to contribute to all aspects of university life.'

Example 4: Philosophy

Question 1: *Why do you want to study this course or subject?*

I first encountered Philosophy in Year 8, in a Religious Studies lesson, when we looked at Plato's Cave, retold in Stephen Law's The Philosophy Files. The questions and methods in philosophy fascinated me, but I realised I also had an aptitude for embracing and untangling them. The allegory was an important way of understanding what I later learnt to be a distinction between appearance and reality. Bombarded with information, where social media was feeling like a whole other world, it gave me a great deal of comfort to know that there was a way to distinguish between appearance and reality, and that philosophy offered me a personal academic pathway. Many people never think about the difference between appearance and reality, and they assume that things are pretty much as they seem to be, and for those things outside of the range of their perception or thought, well those things might not well exist. I was obviously not one of those people.

I became gripped by the questions of personal identity after encountering the 'controversial and falsidical' Ship of Theseus Paradox. I read Reasons and Persons by Derek Parfit, as well as the David Edmonds Biography of Parfit. I was struck by what a strange, dislocated life some academics and philosophers led, but also how I didn't think personal identity can simply consist of psychological continuity either in a traditional Lockean or Parfitean sense. I discovered that my difficulties with this idea was already referred to as the circularity objection. I worried about how dislocated some accounts of personhood were and how they seemed to be removed from the 'reality' of everyday lives, and so found it refreshing to see accounts from Maya Schechtman in her paper 'Personal and Personal Identity.' I love that philosophy can hold together in a single focus both the abstract and the concrete, particulars and the whole and that the conceptual is also the practical and that conceptual understanding have very real-life implications when we consider the concept of who or what is a person.

2,051 characters

Question 2: *How have your qualifications and studies helped you to prepare for this course or subject?*

A level English Literature has been a strong complement to my Religious Studies: Philosophy and Ethics A level, in that the disciplines are often referred to as bedfellows. I am used to reading extensively and producing essays that evince depth and synthesis. I adore the work of Iris Murdoch, and have come to see so many novels and films in a Murdochian sense – in that they so often speak to universal concerns. I was shortlisted for the RIP Think Essay Competition and my essay on response to a question on Plato's Cave used a Murdochian interpretation of the Cave allegory. I have completed a MOOC led by the University of York on logical form and the use of truth tables. I am also part of the school debate and Philosothon teams.

Mathematics and Philosophy both incorporate a strive of logical and coherent systems. I achieved a Silver in the UKMT Senior Challenge. I undertook an EPQ that combined my interest in philosophy, literature and mental health. I explored the role of narrativity for mental health recovery and whether this narration was, in fact, helpful to the patient. The undertaking of such a complicated and controversial interdisciplinary study allowed me to make more complex nuanced arguments and to undertake and understand the all-encompassing nature of extensive research.

1,301 characters

Question 3: *What else have you done to prepare outside of education, and why are these experiences useful?*

I'd like to springboard from philosophy into a career in the media and found it inspiring when Ione Wells, Foreign Correspondent for BBC News, came to speak at our school and said how her Philosophy A level was her most useful A level, as it allowed her to quickly understand, present and analyse complex arguments. I helped to set up an academic journal at my school called SOPHIA and have loved writing for, and being on the editorial board, for the publication.

I enjoy netball and athletics and as part of my school's first teams I have learned leadership and teamwork. I also enjoy debating and can present a compelling and logical argument.

645 characters

TOTAL: 3,997 characters

Commentary on Example 4

Question 1

This personal statement is particularly effective at building a narrative and simply having an advanced style of writing. It was engaging, from the perspective of the reader, to almost join the applicant on their journey, learning more about the origins of a deep curiosity for, in this case, the study of philosophy. One of the early sentences very much hit home in terms of offering a true taste of how the applicant could be a fantastic fit for the university course: 'The questions and methods in philosophy fascinated me, but I realised I also had an aptitude for embracing and untangling them.' In the same way, as we saw with the Economics example, the applicant here has been able to identify a particular theme – in this case, the intriguing philosophical topic of appearance and reality. (The Economics example used gold.) Moreover, the philosophical topic has been lifted to modern times, offering contemporary societal examples where this topic could manifest, namely, the bombardment of social media. Another way in which we can ascertain that this university course could be a good fit is that the applicant has clearly stated so: '. . . philosophy offered me a personal academic pathway'. We see an engaging short sentence further heighten the intrigue for the reader, wanting to ascertain more about this candidate, where there was some reflection on the duality/juggling of appearance and reality, that people may think about, followed by the sharp and snappy response being that 'I was obviously not one of those people'. What we can take away from the opening paragraph is that one should not necessarily shy away from being overt and direct in highlighting why this subject is such a good fit for them. In addition, it is effective to be creative – find your niche area of academic interest and build this into the overall narrative of self-marketing while ensuring that the writing is of both high quality and engaging for the reader.

The second paragraph showcases a fantastic balance between showcasing some relevant super-curricular experiences (e.g. relevant wider reading) and not just describing what was covered but indeed going beyond this with some reflections and critical analysis. If you are a student reading this, you will be aware that often the higher bands of the mark scheme in exam answers (especially for social science and humanities subjects) require evaluation. Equally, if you are a member of staff holding a postgraduate degree, you'll perhaps recall university lectures often highlighting that the difference between 'undergrad' and 'postgrad' is the ability to really offer a nuanced analysis and evaluation – that is, a deeper level of critical thinking. While, as mentioned previously, the personal statement is by no means an academic essay, often the more refined and overall higher-level personal statements will offer interesting analysis of some relevant subject material. Therefore, I would really encourage all personal statement writers to ensure that they have considered interspersing a few reflective/evaluative points where possible. This really elevates the tone and is a flashing light to admissions tutors that you have a lot to offer their university as a future student. If you are insightful here, then you may well contribute to seminar discussions, for example. A moment where this balance of describing and analysing comes into play is where the applicant named and lightly described several pieces of academic literature and then went in with an evaluative reflection: 'I was struck by what a strange, dislocated life some academics and philosophers led, but also how I didn't think personal identity can simply consist of psychological continuity either in a traditional Lockean or Parfitean sense.' We can identify that the applicant is engaging with the material – digesting this and then sharing some insightful views on the back of this. Furthermore, another highlight was to see some reflection but also a certain affirmation that Philosophy is the right course as there is a palpable passion: 'I love that philosophy can hold together in a single focus both the abstract and the concrete . . .' Be bold in sharing your passion.

Question 2

As often mentioned in suggestions for Question 2, you should not be listing your qualifications and studies but should use what you have learned and enjoyed to amplify your skills and experiences – of course, within an academic context. The applicant carefully considered which qualities are useful for the university course (Philosophy in this case) and crafted some angles in which these qualities could be addressed. A poignant example of this is in the statement: 'I am used to reading extensively and producing essays that evince depth and synthesis.' Note how not necessarily all current qualifications/studies were mentioned in equal measure, but the applicant selected only two A levels to address in particular (English Literature and Religious Studies: Philosophy and Ethics) while giving a small nod to Mathematics. Again, Question 2 is not an exhaustive list and so you can be à la carte and thus selective.

As we see in this example, super-curricular content can also be used in Question 2. Generally, it'll be the kind of super-curricular which is less experiential (e.g. work experience) and more along the lines of theoretical in nature (e.g. an essay competition). This is a fine line, and what's more important is that you successfully link the super-curricular experience with your studies (the focus of this question). Here, the applicant included an essay competition and an online course, what is often referred to as a massive open online course (MOOC). There was also the mention of debating.

This example is particularly heavy on super-curricular activities for a Question 2, highlighting that there are no necessarily correct or incorrect approaches as to where you write about these activities. Again, this reminds us of the point that the personal statement will indeed be read as a whole rather than being read and judged in isolated sections. The second paragraph includes an academic competition and the Extended Project Qualification (EPQ).

Certainly, applicants do not need to take an EPQ. However, it can be useful to have and is absolutely worth writing about within the personal statement. I am very often asked by students whether the EPQ has to be connected to their future university aspirations. Can, for example, a medical applicant complete an EPQ project writing 5,000 words about a seemingly unrelated history topic? The answer is that either is fine. Writing about an unrelated topic highlights your wider interests and roundedness as a candidate; offering research on your university subject area amplifies your academic curiosity and knowledge of a possibly a niche area. The reason I wanted to mention this is that the EPQ provides relevant transferable skills for university study, which actually is the main point and thus it is less of a consideration as to what you choose to focus on. The applicant here identified a key benefit of the EPQ, being that it '. . . allowed me to make more complex nuanced arguments and to undertake and understand the all-encompassing nature of extensive research'. Transferable skills such as these are useful additions when marketing yourself and showcasing how your educational experiences have prepared you for the next step of your studies. As a rule of thumb, if pushed, I would say choose a topic related to your university subject (as you have both the transferability and relevant subject material). However, if you have a particular interest that you would like to pursue that is not related to your university subject, why not go for it! An EPQ is a long piece of work and you need to stay motivated to be dedicated – so choose your topic wisely!

Question 3

It is not essential to link how the degree you hope to complete in the future will lead to a future career or further study. Nevertheless, if you do have a clear vision that you would like to include and that offers an interesting opportunity to write more, then you certainly can mention what this might be. In this example, the applicant would like to use Philosophy as a platform to secure a role within the media. The applicant then went on to provide an interesting example of a guest speaker from the media who talked about the benefit of Philosophy, albeit at A level for this instance rather than degree level. This provided some stimulating discussion and was a great segue into then bringing in the experience of setting up and maintaining a school journal. Question 3 is certainly the place for any extra-curriculars (e.g. sports, hobbies, music and other non-academic interests). Here, the applicant included netball and athletics, also pointing to the benefits of leadership and teamwork skills being enhanced as a by-product. There was some repetition with Question 2 and Question 3, which was the mention of debates. Remember that you only have a limited character count of 4,000 and that the piece will be read as a whole. However, there could have been a separation between academic debates (e.g. the Philosothon) and more general debates less connected to philosophy. Some minor repetition, if you have key skills or experiences that you would like to drive home, can be effective. Just keep in mind that there is a character count and so you should be as economical and strategic as possible!

Example 5: Architecture

Question 1: *Why do you want to study this course or subject?*

Growing up I've always enjoyed travelling. When I was 14 I remember visiting Brazil's capital and being fascinated by its futuristic architectural designs inspired by modernism. Observing the National Congress of Brazil, the Cathedral of Brasília, and the residence of the President offered glimpses into a forward looking Brazil and elements of modern design where I contemplated how I could utilise this imaginative creativity myself to inform a changing world, especially in a time of climate change, wars, alongside positive development progress. Such structures which were made of glass and concrete and defined by sharp edges and symmetrical lines, piquing my curiosity for the subject of Architecture.

In turn, I decided to read 'How Buildings Learn' by Stewart Brand. This book spoke about the evolution of buildings overtime, exploring how buildings need to adapt and be dynamic spaces as needs evolve. This got me to think about the role of structures not just from an aesthetic perspective but also got me to consider the adaptability and usefulness of buildings. This struck me as being a crucial part of challenges the world currently faces, particularly as economic activities in different countries develop and climate patterns change. At university I would be drawn to learning more around such modules to do with related topics such as sustainable housing alongside design and policy related to the rise of Artificial Intelligence, all topics needed to understand futuristic architectures which are not only aesthetic but also practical in a dynamic world.

I endeavour to become a chartered architect, with a focus on sustainable design to solve challenges the world currently faces. I'm especially interested in adaptive reuse and how architecture can lower its environmental impact while benefitting communities. I hope to one day work on large scale international projects across the globe.

1,908 characters

Question 2: *How have your qualifications and studies helped you to prepare for this course or subject?*

To prepare for advanced Architectural studies, my A Level in Art has enabled me to perfect my eye for visual detail and expand my drawing technique, which will be useful when considering the creation of architectural plans. The course allowed me to undertake architectural sketching, model-making, and use CAD software like SketchUp. I've also studied A Levels in Maths and Physics, which both have exposed me to thinking more analytically and logically when solving quantitative problems. In my Extended Project Qualification, I evaluated the evolution of sustainable urban design in Brazil's capital, based upon my past travel interests, developing my analytical research skills. I also completed an online Udemy course in 'How a Building is Designed and

Built', which provided me with a useful applied knowledge of the role of architects in structural design. Such studies allowed me to develop skills which will be useful for this course at university but also reinforce my desire to undertake this degree.

Moreover, I participated in the week-long Bartlett Summer School at UCL during my summer. I was able to comprehend the importance of architecture as a collaborative practice and particularly enjoyed the end of course mini-exhibition where we were able to showcase our design work. I engaged with UCL's own education department building where I reviewed its design and tweaked it to engage with one which was better adapted to cope with future practicalities and nature in a modernistic style, which you can see submitted within my portfolio work.

1,556 characters

Question 3: *What else have you done to prepare outside of education, and why are these experiences useful?*

Outside of education I maintain a sketchbook and enjoy photographing buildings during my visits across the UK but also to other countries. I regularly visit exhibitions at the Tate Modern in London where I seek inspiration for design practice and principles. I also lead my school's Art Club, which taught me to collaboratively work with others and the importance of organisation, a key skill Architecture students need.

420 characters

TOTAL: 3,884 characters

Commentary on Example 5

Question 1

What is particularly unique about this personal statement example, compared to the other five in this book, is that the majority of super-curricular activities are actually found outside of Question 1. In accordance with what has been suggested in this book, there is the recommended total of super-curricular examples (eight), but Question 1 has the least number, whereas I would usually recommend that the majority of super-curricular material falls into this question. What this example highlights is that there are multiple ways to structure a strong UCAS personal statement, and it is crucial to remember that the three questions will be read as a single piece and so it is more important to ensure that the content is included rather than considering exactly where it has been placed (while still ensuring that the original question has been addressed).

It is considered a cliché to use phrases such as 'I've always enjoyed', so this could possibly be rephrased, especially considering that this was the opening sentence of Question 1. Having said this, what would make this phrase more of a cliché would be for the applicant to write, 'I have always enjoyed Architecture'. Should that have been the case, it would have very much downgraded the impact of the opening paragraph. Instead, what the applicant here has done is to specifically link this not directly to the subject but to the enjoyment of travel. Moreover, what is very much not a cliché, and is a good hallmark of an attention-grabbing personal statement, is to then expand on a personal anecdote. In this case, the anecdote being a visit to Brazil and then some name-dropping of notable buildings and an interesting reflection, which demonstrates a deep passion and academic curiosity for the chosen university course of Architecture.

The applicant goes on to link some wider reading with a relevant book (this book has been widely listed by universities on their recommended reading lists) and offers some interesting reflection – amplifying that this has been digested in detail and that there is a genuine interest in the subject. What particularly stood out for me was that there was a sentence focused on what the applicant would like to do at university, starting with 'At university, I would be drawn to . . .' While it is not possible to know all of what is available to learn at university or the experiences to be had, it can be effective to share some insights into what you would be particularly drawn to. Of course, be strategic. It would be less useful to name modules or specific topics that may be less popular or not available at your selected universities (based on reading the course page and possibly researching the academic staff there), but if there are common areas that you are particularly excited by, then it could be a very nice touch to indicate this. It shows the admissions tutors that the applicant is motivated and has done their research to therefore know that this is a good fit institution. Back in Chapter 5, I mentioned the importance of cross-referencing a full draft of the personal statement with specific university course pages for final inspiration. Moreover, showing what you can gain from university study makes it easier for the admissions tutor to identify that you will be motivated and thus an asset to the institution, making you a good choice candidate.

Question 2

The answer for Question 2 starts with a description of how the current A level subjects offer good preparation for the university course. In this case, drawing technique, use of relevant software, as well as analytical and logical thinking. Earlier today, I was delivering a personal statement support class, and initially students found Question 2 tricky – namely, in terms of identifying how their subjects link to the university course. As we can see in this example, there doesn't have to be a huge amount of writing on the specific A levels (or other pre-university education) and their link to university. Here, for example, it was only the first 74 words/489 characters. Consider several important skills, attributes and/or qualities relevant for the university course, and then consider how your subjects have enhanced these. Provide some examples, if possible. The majority of this question was focused on super-curricular content (172 words/1,066 characters). Again, this demonstrates that Question 1 and Question 2 can both involve relevant super-curricular material.

Question 3

Absolutely, here we can see that this question, while this is generally a section geared more towards extra-curricular, still contains super-curricular content. I think much of the reason for this is that Architecture does require experiences linked with artistic overtones and so activities that often are considered hobbies (e.g. photography and visiting galleries) apply. These experiences tick the boxes in terms of showcasing the applicant's ability for the applicant to possess qualities that can enhance the social fabric of the university. While this is a very good personal statement, I think it could have been enhanced by offering a 'true' extra-curricular less connected to a direct link with Architecture (e.g. sports, music, dance, cooking, etc.). It is rare to see in high-quality personal statements, but there is still roughly 100 characters left to use. Final drafts should really be 3,980 and above to be as close as possible to the 4,000 maximum. Therefore, there was adequate space to consider an additional extra-curricular or even more space that could have been used for the other questions.

Example 6: Computer Science

Question 1: *Why do you want to study this course or subject?*

My passion for computer science began at 16 when a guest speaker, invited by my maths and physics teacher, shared how his degree enabled him to create an app connecting surplus food from shops to consumers at reduced prices. His innovation tackled food waste and became a global success, showing how technology can drive meaningful change. He stressed how data-sharing improves societal well-being and the importance of mathematics in programming. Motivated, I strengthened my skills through reading Riley and Warner's (2021) 'Essential Pre-University Mathematics for Sciences' and by solving online problems.

At the same time, I was learning in history how misinformation, like belief in the miasma theory, delayed medical progress. This deepened my understanding of how crucial reliable data is, whether in healthcare, public policy, or technology. I began to see computer science as a powerful tool to support better decision-making across fields.

To build my knowledge, I completed Harvard's year-long online Data Science course, learning Python, SQL, Pandas, NumPy, Matplotlib, and machine learning with Scikit-learn. For my final project, I analysed commuter data to improve traffic light timings and reduce congestion. I further honed my skills during a summer school, in Oxford, where I modelled bacteriotaxis – the motion of bacteria. I wrote a Python simulation exploring the effects of antibacterial agents and magnetic fields on mobility. The instructor praised the project for its originality and research potential.

A hospital stay made this even more personal. I saw how diagnostic software supported medical professionals. This led me to complete a one-year IBM course in AI, where I studied machine learning, natural language processing, ethical AI, and real-world applications. My final project involved designing a chatbot that directed patients to hospitals based on wait times and needs.

These experiences inspired me to specialize in AI and machine learning for diagnostics, while also supporting pro bono initiatives like local charities, something I have already begun as a volunteer webmaster. Ultimately, I hope to become a computer scientist who not only drives innovation but uses it to create positive, responsible change – just as I was inspired to do at 16.

2,284 characters

Question 2: *How have your qualifications and studies helped you to prepare for this course or subject?*

Attending Liceo Classico has provided me with a well-rounded education, blending sciences (maths, physics, biology, chemistry) with humanities (Italian, English, Latin, Ancient Greek, history, and philosophy). This diverse curriculum has strengthened my analytical and problem-solving skills, essential in computer science. In my final three years, I pursued an extra computer science course, gaining both theoretical knowledge and hands-on programming experience, which will be invaluable in my university studies and career.

My scientific background helps me understand complex computational models, while humanities have sharpened my logical thinking through structured reasoning in ancient languages and deepened my awareness of technology's societal impact. Additionally, humanities have refined my communication skills, crucial for presenting ideas and collaborating with diverse teams.

Beyond school, I expanded my technical expertise through two edX courses in cybersecurity and web programming. I applied these skills as a webmaster for my local World Wildlife Fund branch, redesigning their website for better security and functionality. My contributions led to increased site visits and fewer hacking attempts, demonstrating the real-world impact of programming.

1,271 characters

Question 3: *What else have you done to prepare outside of education, and why are these experiences useful?*

I am a black belt in karate and an instructor. Training since childhood has instilled discipline and resilience – qualities essential in both sports and computer science. Developing efficient code requires persistence and problem-solving, much like mastering karate. As an instructor, I learned to communicate complex ideas clearly, a skill that translates into coding; just as I break down techniques, well-documented code ensures usability.

442 characters

TOTAL: 3,997 characters

Commentary on Example 6

Question 1

Subject passion and academic curiosity for the university course, in this case, Computer Science, ooze throughout Question 1. There were two examples of personal anecdotes the application reflected on to highlight a deep interest in computer science. The first example was in the introduction, drawing upon the moment a guest speaker shared his experiences of creating a smartphone application. The second personal anecdote came in the form of a hospital stay and observing diagnostic software, which then led to completing a one-year course with IBM. The example of the second anecdote shows us that such personal anecdotes do not just need to be placed within the introduction to immediately grab the attention of the reader, but can feature in other parts of the personal statement too. The crystallising moment of realising that Computer Science is the right course to pursue at university could have come in the form of the hospital stay as much as it could in the guest speaker's talk. Both would have been relevant and interesting. So, if you are a student with multiple personal anecdotes of crystallising moments, it is useful to know that these are not necessarily mutually exclusive and so both can feature within your personal statement. Moreover, the second anecdote was particularly effective – being in the hospital could well seem like an unrelated situation in terms of its connection to computer science, and yet the applicant was able to find a relevant link and make a connection (observing practical applications with the diagnostic software). This, from the perspective of the reader, reinforces the message of the applicant being driven and motivated to pursue this university course.

My general recommendation is to have roughly six super-curricular activities featured in Question 1. In this personal statement example, we have exactly six activities (the guest speaker; wider reading; an online Harvard course; a summer school; IBM course; volunteering as a webmaster). What's also worth noting is the impressive variety of super-curricular experiences. With the exception of the Harvard and IBM courses, all of these activities are particularly different to one another. Variety is key for amplifying a breadth of knowledge and experience – thus further enhancing a sense of academic passion, curiosity and suitability for the chosen university course. The applicant rightly identified an important skill relevant to Computer Science (proficiency in computer languages) and so ensured that the experience of writing a Python simulation was included. When preparing to write a personal statement and building a portfolio of super-curricular activities, a useful exercise could be to check university course pages and other subject-specific resources to help identify useful and relevant experiences. Modelling the motion of bacteria sounds like a rather unique experience which enables this personal statement to further standout by being different and thus memorable. Where possible, avoid cliché super-curricular examples by sourcing unique experiences and/or reflecting on them in novel ways. Looking at the summer school experience, note that this is not a UK-based applicant and so while visiting the UK before making an application is not essential by any means; the fact that this applicant has invested time and other resources to visit Oxford reinforces the notion of being motivated and dedicated to studying in the UK. This could be a nice touch for international applicants, wherever possible, to hint at some form of previous exposure or interest in the UK.

As outlined in the introduction and the first paragraph of the main body, there is a common theme/topic. This is the importance of reliable data sharing. Identifying relevant themes and topics could help personal statement writers to construct a structure to develop a dialogue and organise super-curricular content. Staying on the structure, it was particularly effective to see a rounding off between the introductory paragraph and the conclusion of Question 1 – referring back to the main academic spark for Computer Science at the age of 16. While, from the perspective of the applicant, being aged 16 may only be one or two years before making an undergraduate application and so doesn't seem that long ago. Nevertheless, it is always better to pinpoint a specific moment as opposed to using phrases such as 'I have always been interested in . . .' or 'Since I can remember . . .', 'Since a young age . . .' and so on.

Question 2

Conventional guidance, especially for those completing pre-university qualifications that are common in the UK (e.g. A levels, Scottish Highers and the International Baccalaureate), is to avoid listing subjects and thus wasting important character space on information that the university already has from your UCAS application outside of the personal statement. However, you certainly can list specific subjects to help you set the scene or underpin a particular point. In this case, the applicant wanted to show the breadth and blend between the sciences and humanities as good preparation for Computer Science.

Moreover, as a non-UK-based applicant, the Italian Liceo Classico form of education may well be less known to some personal statement readers. This is not to say that universities are unaware of education systems outside the UK – far from it, in fact. You can read about non-UK educational requirements, such as predicted grades and specific subjects, on university course pages online, for example. Nevertheless, giving overview information about your studies, as a non-UK applicant, will be useful.

The applicant here has done particularly well at selecting specific parts of their pre-university education and selling himself as to how this education has enhanced relevant skills in preparation for the course at university. For example: 'My scientific background helps me understand complex computational models, while humanities have sharpened my logical thinking through structured reasoning . . .' This helps the admissions tutor identify that the applicant has thoroughly researched the university course and is prepared for the next step to university.

While Question 1 will, in most cases, contain the bulk of super-curricular activities, it is a nice touch to include a few more for good measure in Question 2. In this example, at first glance, it appears that the applicant has used space at the end of this question to expand some more on super-curricular activities mentioned in Question 1 (two courses and the webmaster volunteering). In general, it is not effective to reinstate previously mentioned information in another question as universities have indicated that the personal statement will be read and assessed as a single piece of text and so parts should not be repeated. However, with this example, there is new information and some useful expansion to enrich what has previously been discussed. So, in this case, it has been effective. Upon second glance, the two courses mentioned could well be different, as indicated by their topics (cybersecurity and web programming). Therefore, to help guide the reader, the applicant could have made this clearer, perhaps by starting with 'In addition to my courses with Harvard and IBM, I also . . .' It is not all about quantity, but if you have different activities to include, ensure that these are considered as such. Why miss out!

Question 3

This Question 3 example does particularly well at showing us that there are not necessarily many extra-curricular or additional experiences required to write an interesting, engaging and ultimately effective piece. Here, the example of karate has been applied to amplify a roundedness of personal skills and qualities in addition to an awareness and preparedness for Computer Science. Admissions tutors, therefore, are able to see that the applicant not only comes with a good academic background but also has more to offer irrespective of the course. The applicant drew upon discipline, resilience, problem-solving and communication. It is certainly fine to include multiple activities and experiences, should applicants have these that they feel are suitable to share, as seen in other model personal statements presented in this chapter.

As readers of this book will know, each personal statement question has a 350 minimum character limit. I would recommend devoting most of the character space to Question 1 and Question 2 and roughly 10% of the space to Question 3. This applicant has kept it short and in line with the 10%, coming in at 11% with 442 characters.

www.ingramcontent.com/pod-product-compliance
Lightning Source LLC
Chambersburg PA
CBHW052101230426
43662CB00036B/1728